Praise for #1 Bestselling Author Joe Bovino's First Book, Field Guide to Chicks of the United States

Judge, 2013 Global eBook Awards (Gold Medal, Humor)
"The illustrations were fantastic. The book was hilarious. I laughed through the whole thing (and I'm a chick... LOL)."

Tamazon, Night Owls Reviews (Top Pick)
"Field Guide to Chicks of the United States by Joe Bovino is a hilarious look into the women of the USA. If you like people watching and commenting I can say you need to check this book out today. You and your friends will want to read this together for the most laughs... My husband and I enjoyed this book. For those who don't find this hilarious feel free to seek your comedy somewhere else."

Kimberly McClain Cardenas 5 of 5 stars – Goodreads.com
"I won this from Goodreads.com. This is a seriously funny although fairly spot on kind of book. It is very straight forward and not for those who take offense to stereotypes. Yes even a girl like me was represented almost to a tee. I am sending it next to my brother so he can pick and choose his next girlfriend a little more carefully next time and with a lot more knowledge behind him."

Colleen Schilinski 5 of 5 stars – Goodreads.com
"This was a great book. It's funny and all my guy friends want to borrow it. I'll have to put my information on the inside of this book, so I get it back. It is a must read for anyone, because Joe Bovino did a great job telling us the way it is about woman in different city's all across the United States. I even have quite a few pages marked for future

references, and to show certain men in my life. This is definitely a GOODREAD for me."

Baniva 5.0 out of 5 stars – Amazon.com
"I'm gay and I love it! This book is so funny, I met Joe at an event and he told me about his masterpiece. I was a little hesitant at first but I decided to go ahead and buy one! It is painfully accurate as I was able to match up some characteristics of my girlfriends to their cartoon counterparts. It's the most genius thing ever. Loved it so much I bought another for a friend who I consider a connoisseur of the 'female species'!"

Marissa 5.0 out of 5 stars – Amazon.com
"This book is hilarious! Not to miss, easy read, light hearted and will make you laugh. Everyone might be a little thrown off at first, some maybe offended, but once you actually read it you will see the humor and love it. Not only is it a great convo starter and even better gift, but it is the written out guide to chicks...! Read, compare and enjoy. Guys will love it and girls too... Definitely recommend it for good laughs and fun. Find out who you are ladies and guys, your "dream" girl awaits... Well done and I look forward to sharing this book with friends."

Arktik Fitness "Michelle" (Juneau AK) 5.0 out of 5 stars – Amazon.com
"So Glad I Downloaded! Starting reading last night & was worried about waking the husband up with my laughing! Irreverent, hilarious & spot on in some spooky ways :) You've done your research Joe!"

bitchology

Truth and Lies about
Who Men Love and Marry

JOE BOVINO

Four-Time #1 Bestselling Author

Chickspotting, LLC

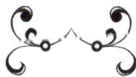

Notice

Dedication

To the women in my family. Thanks for showing me how great American women can be and for loving me even when I'm a pain in the butt. I love you with all my heart and always will.

I'd also like to thank you, the one holding this book and reading this line, for your interest in the study of bitches and the truth about who men love and marry. I sincerely hope this book makes a difference for you and wish you all the best.

Contents

Introduction

"Watch any sitcom, commercial, movie comedy, the go-to punch line is always the tight-ass, limp-dick, Dockers-wearing, tiny penis, bland-food eating, white guy. White men can't jump. They can't dance. They can't fuck... Really?"

— BILL MAHER, *REAL TIME WITH BILL MAHER: BEIGE AGAINST THE MACHINE* (HBO), 4/22/16.

Sherry Argov's perennial #1 bestselling book for women on dating and mate seeking, *Why Men Love Bitches: From Doormat to Dreamgirl—A Woman's Guide to Holding Her Own in a Relationship*, has been sending the wrong message to American women at the worst possible time. That book, with a lie for a title, is a wrecking ball. As a public service, she should retitle it *Why Men Loathe and Leave Bitches: from Doormat to Dipshit—A Feminist's Guide to Holding Him in Contempt*, but she won't because her sales would tank.

Bitchology doesn't play silly word games or engage in feminist groupthink. This is a tough-love relationship guide for women who think they're too nice or too bitchy to succeed with men and who haven't abandoned common sense. It demonstrates that the choice between being a submissive doormat and a man-hating bitch is a false one. You lose either way, but there's another approach that works like a charm.

Men with options in an increasingly global dating market are looking for a different kind of woman—a *confidently feminine* one or "Keeper"—and Keepers are in short supply in many parts of the country.

That thesis should come as encouraging news to most of you, but it's not as easy as it seems. Perfection isn't necessary, of course, but you normally won't change your luck with men in a meaningful way by being confident or feminine. You need an abundance of both—confidence and femininity—to really crush it out there.

How do I know and who am I to provide guidance on this subject? The short answer is: I'm a nice guy—arguably too nice—who's been-there-done-that when it comes to dating and relationships short of marriage, has always liked women, and cares enough about you to write this book and take the heat from some of the most vile feminists on the planet. I've also been blessed with amazing parents, grandparents, younger sisters, and loyal friends, including women of all kinds whom I've had the pleasure of dating and getting to know over the years in the United States and abroad.

After working as a lawyer and international business consultant for twenty years, I decided to do something completely different—write a book. I ultimately chose to write about women from different American subcultures because I wanted to write about something that I loved and could speak about authoritatively. The project also appealed to me because, after so many years of practicing law in a stressful environment, I wanted to write something humorous, and many of the funniest and most interesting stories of my life dealt with women, dating and relationships.

So I resigned from the full-time practice of law in 2008 and spent the next four and half years researching and writing my first book, *Field Guide to Chicks of the United States*, which went on to win a gold medal for humor in the 2013 Global eBook Awards and eventually become an Amazon #1 bestseller. I knew that the book wouldn't appeal to some people and included a disclaimer in the introduction, but I didn't anticipate how vicious and unscrupulous my critics would be before the book even came out.

Most notably, more than four months before the book was published or otherwise available to read, Lindy West (whom I'd never heard of before) published a blog post in *Jezebel* entitled "The 92 'Species' of

Women According to an Incredibly Stupid Dude from a P90X Video," wherein she labeled my book "Sexist Garbage," "Creepy," and racist. The following day, Emma Gray, Executive Women's Editor at *Huff Post Women*, piled on with a column entitled, wait for it... "Joe Bovino's 'Field Guide to Chicks of the United States' May Be Worst Book Ever." That's right, Gray hadn't read the book either but thought it might be worse than *Mein Kampf*.

Two years later, after my book had received rave reviews from actual readers of both sexes, West apparently persuaded her then-colleague at *Jezebel*, Erin Gloria Ryan, to publish blog posts based on my field-guide concept and research, without attribution, entitled "The United States of Bros: A Map and Field Guide" and "The United States of Basic Bitches: A Map and Field Guide," which were later recognized as two of the "100 Most Popular Jezebel Posts of 2014." Neither of Ryan's cringeworthy rip-offs mentioned my book or West's article disparaging it and me in *Jezebel* in the recent past. It was unethical and appallingly hypocritical, but it exposed my feminist critics as frauds, cowards—West should have had the balls to do the dirty work herself—and white-male-hating bitches.

Late last year, I published another book entitled *Chicaspotting: A Field Guide to Latinas of the United States*. It became my first international #1 bestseller on Amazon, but it triggered a new division of militant feminists called "feministas." Ignoring the humor, cultural insights, and complimentary observations in my book, these Northeastern nutjobs initiated a campaign to *ban* it like a bunch of Nazis. They obsessed over my race in their articles, including my personal favorite from *Latina Magazine* entitled "This Sexist and Racist White Guy Writes Books That Degrade Latinas." Then their readers, like lemmings, sunk the book's rating on Amazon with a slew of phony 1-star reviews.

I can shrug off the smears and character assassination because no one who knows me well would call me sexist, racist or homophobic with a straight face, and my books can speak for themselves with or without support from these buffoons, but I can't sit silently by while sniveling feminists and social justice warriors deliberately mislead you about American men—especially white, working-class ones—whom they're driving away in droves. They're lying to you, dispensing truly awful advice about dating and relationships, and damaging gender relations in the process. Enough.

This book will examine the devastating impact of third-wave feminism and its attendant bitchiness on America's dysfunctional dating scene. It will explore fourteen subcultures of American and hyphenated-American women as case studies, highlight conspicuous deficiencies in confidence and femininity, and suggest remedial measures. And, in the final chapter, it will introduce fifteen "Keeper Principles" to help you become even more of a confidently feminine Keeper who turns the head and wins the heart of a truly great guy.

Truth is, there has never been a better time to be a Keeper in America because men are finding it more difficult than ever to find one. In *Men on Strike: Why Men Are Boycotting Marriage, Fatherhood, and the American Dream—and Why It Matters*, Dr. Helen Smith demonstrates that a shockingly large percentage of single men are simply giving up on love and marriage because American women and society have become so openly hostile and anti-male. It's an outstanding book, but Dr. Smith doesn't go far enough in her critique of American women and misses another unintended consequence of the war on men and masculinity.

America's best men aren't just taking their balls and going home. They're taking a harder look at their options in an increasingly global dating market and rationally choosing to seek out, date, love and marry Keepers—including a rapidly growing number of foreign and hyphenated-American ones—rather than American women who've deluded themselves into believing that bitchiness is cool, helpful, or desirable.

Who are "America's best men?" Well, they're not *actual* misogynists, players, racists, serial liars, criminals, or jerks. There's no excuse for them, and this book won't delve into their twisted psychology. America's best men are good and decent gentlemen, "dream guys," alpha males, bad boys with an upside, eligible bachelors, and other high-quality men with potential to be a great boyfriend, husband, or soulmate, but they're increasingly cynical about American women, and they are suffering from the relationship equivalent of post-traumatic stress disorder after dealing with the worst of them for so long.

That's not to say there aren't Keepers who treat men with love and respect throughout the United States, especially in the traditional South and Midwest, and you may be one of them. (I hope so.) These ladies aren't part of the problem—they're an integral part of the *solution* and serve as role models for other women—but they're not in charge anymore. Repulsive feminists and self-described bitches, cheered on by the media (who love a train wreck), have marginalized America's best women and drowned out their pleasant voices with a pervasive, deafening shrillness.

So, who are these bitches who are chasing all the great guys away and making dating and relationships more difficult for everyone else?

Chapter One tackles that question.

Chapter One

Femininity ≠ Weakness

"She didn't care that people called her a bitch. 'It's just another word for feminist,' she told me with pride."

— GAYLE FORMAN, *IF I STAY*

"Feminism is cancer."

— MILO YIANNOPOULOS,
JOURNALIST AND DANGEROUS FAGGOT

The New Bitch Is the Old Bitch, Only Worse

Let's begin our study of bitches with a dose of reality. Here's what the word "bitch" actually means:

- "a lewd or immoral woman" or "a malicious, spiteful, or overbearing woman" (Merriam-Webster.com);
- "a woman considered to be mean, overbearing, or contemptible" (TheFreeDictionary.com); and
- "the worst species of woman: the Feminus Obnoxium" (Askmen.com).

Men love all kinds of women, but they don't love bitches. They don't even like bitches. No one does. But that's not what third-wave feminists want you to think and believe. They need to convince you that bitchiness is cool, smart, and counterintuitively appealing to men. So, they deliberately mislead anyone who will listen, parrot a demonstrably false narrative, and harm the very women they profess to care about.

Some delusional American bitches actually brag about how easily they attract and abuse nice guys, who allegedly find them irresistible.

Consider Gigi Engle. In her blog post entitled "24 Reasons Nice Guys Always Chase The B*tch – As Told By The B*tch," Engle describes herself as a "rude" (ostensibly white) "Alpha Bitch" with a "huge ego" who "says the meanest things" and "horrible things" to "perfectly nice guys," who respond "like sick puppies" to her "black widow ways" and "bitch-tastic glory."

Engle would have you believe that "ultra-sweet" American guys are "obsessed" with her and other "nasty," "bossy," "volatile," "complex," "elusive and difficult" Alpha Bitches who are "uninterested in what anyone else thinks," "have very little attention and time to devote to [men]," and act like "a complete a-hole." According to Engle, "in some "f*cking twisted" way, these desperate yes-men and "mamas' boys" actually enjoy being "babied and … abused," "second-in-command"

and "slapped around" by bitches from hell. She sums it up this way: "In the end, the nice girls get cats, the boys get their hearts broke and the huge bitch gets the corner office and a martini."

She probably doesn't care that almost everything she writes and believes is wrong, but it is. Alpha Bitches appeal only to pathetically weak men and horny guys who are willing to tolerate their disgusting personalities, appearance and hygiene long enough to get laid, shower up, and leave. You see, Alpha Bitches and social justice warriors may be hard to stomach for more than a few minutes, but they tend to mirror the wildly promiscuous behavior of the same male jerks and players whom they profess to hate.

Sherry Argov, the author of *Why Men Love Bitches*, is coyer than Ms. Engle, but the destructive impact of her book on impressionable American women is far greater. Rather than encourage you to embrace bitchiness for what it is—pure vindictiveness and nastiness—Argov distorts the plain meaning of the word "bitch" beyond all recognition. At one point, she even goes so far as to define a "bitch" as her polar opposite: A nice girl. "A bitch is *nice*. She's sweet as a Georgia peach. She smiles and she is feminine." Then she adds: "Let us conclude... by redefining the word *bitch*. Think of it as a "term of endearment."

Bitch, please.

Even Ms. Engle, as beastly as she is, manages to be honest about the nature of an American bitch and deserves credit for it. Argov, not so much. She prefers to deceive her readers, beginning with this whopper in the introduction of her book:

> "Among the hundreds of interviews I conducted with men for the book, over 90 percent laughed and agreed with the title within the first thirty seconds. Some men chuckled as if their best-kept secret had just been revealed."

Give me a break. What woman in her right mind believes that load of BS? Years of research in connection with my previous books, considerable personal experience, and common sense dictate that the opposite is true. Well over 90 percent of men will tell you that they avoid bitches like the plague. (Actually, I don't have any friends or acquaintances who love bitches, and it's always been that way. I know a few guys who married bitches, but they didn't realize it at the time.) The rest are morons, pussies or freaks who aren't worth your time... or mine. Frankly, you shouldn't need me to tell you this.

Duping women into believing that men secretly love bitches is bad enough, but Argov doesn't stop there. She encourages her readers to become a "High-Maintenance Bitch," as if it's some kind of an achievement:

> "The only higher crown, the only higher honor, is to be called a "High-Maintenance Bitch." It's a sign of success, indicating that this is the woman the guy ends up keeping. If nothing else, he keeps her for the very practical reason that he's invested so much that he can't let her go."

That is truly barf-worthy advice, ladies. No man wants to attract, get or keep a high-maintenance bitch, and it doesn't take a rocket scientist to know why. Is it any wonder that so many guys are looking for foreign and hyphenated-American Keepers when so many misguided American women actually believe this drivel?

By this point, you may be saying that none of this matters because Argov is surely just kidding around. She's using the word "bitch" in a playful, tongue-in-cheek way to mean something vaguely positive, like a strong, independent woman, a nice girl with a backbone, or... whatever. Well, I can appreciate attempts at humor, and they can't all be winners, but shouldn't men be in on the joke? She apparently doesn't think so:

"If that fateful day ever does arrive when he tells you that you are a bitch? Stop, and take a deep breath. Then enjoy the moment. Smile internally as you say to yourself, 'Okay. Now I know he *truly* does love me.'"

Uh, no. When a man calls you a bitch to your face, he's almost always using the plain meaning of the word, not Argov's meaningless redefinition, and that's nothing to smile about.

Then Argov really exposes herself.

What should American women who are "too nice" *do* to become a bitch-who's-not-really-a-bitch? Well, of course: Look, talk and act more like the *dictionary* definition of a bitch—that is, more like Ms. Engle.

Yep, after all of her word games and inside jokes, Argov's new bitch is the old bitch—only more delusional, willfully blind, or shameless:

- A bitch "understands—and adheres to—the first law of nature: Every animal for herself." (WTF? What is this, a cage match? To quote Thomas Hobbes, life doesn't have to be "solitary, poor, nasty, brutish, and short," Argov.)
- "Just remember, it isn't about a man... Do things when it is convenient, especially if it regards your relationship of choice and who you let in on the 'inside.'" (Rubbish)
- "The bitch never tries that hard to make an impression." (And it shows.)
- Women should develop "irreverence... for what other people think" because a bitch "doesn't try to live up to anyone else's standards—only her own." (This isn't total BS, but be careful. My father always told me not to be a "People Pleaser," so I agree that none of us should go through life trying to please others and live up to someone else's standards. However, if you want to a great guy to love and marry you, don't bury your

head in the sand and act like what he thinks or wants doesn't matter. Would you want him to act that way toward you? No, I didn't think so.)

- "The bitch... gives a very different message. ' Who I am is enough. Take it or leave it.'" (Then, he leaves.)
- "A woman... demeans herself when she compares herself to another woman." (This is just another mind-fuck. We all compare ourselves to other people in certain ways, and it's not demeaning as long as you appreciate who you are as a unique individual.)
- "Any time a woman competes with another woman, she demeans herself." (If you don't compete, you can't lose, right? Wrong.)
- A woman shouldn't "kill herself to impress anyone." (Suicide isn't necessary, but not trying to make a good impression is the best way not to make one.)
- A woman shouldn't cook for her man because cooking is "one of the many ways that women overcompensate." (This is absurd. Argov is clearly a lousy cook–and lay, no doubt–who has no business telling Keepers who enjoy cooking for their men that they shouldn't do it.)
- "Being sassy means you won't knock yourself out." (Men prefer non-sassy Keepers to lazy, worthless, sassy bitches, but otherwise this is good advice.)
- "A bitch doesn't rely on [a particular miniskirt, a belly ring, or a black dress with a plunging neckline] to feel good about herself. She relies on *who she is as a woman*." (Why can't you rely on who you are as a woman and a great outfit to feel good about yourself? It's true that what's on the inside really counts—that goes for all of us—but there's nothing wrong about feeling good when you look good. This is envy masked

as advice, ladies. Argov sees other women feeling good about themselves wearing a beautiful outfit and doesn't like it because she's insecure about her appearance, doesn't get the same positive response from men, or both.)

- "If he tells [a bitch that] he doesn't like red lipstick, she wears it anyway, if it makes her feel good." (Good plan, dumbass.)
- A bitch should "throw a little weight around" and "put him in his place once in a while..." (Are we still talking about love and romance here? Would you want a man to treat you that way in a relationship? No, I didn't think so.)

What's Argov really trying to say with her little nuggets of wisdom? Screw him. Screw her. Screw everybody! Do whatever the hell you want and men will love and marry you.

Here's the problem with that horrible attitude: There's no "reverse magnet" for bitches like Argov and Engle in the real world. Women who believe this nonsense can't compete with Keepers who make an effort to look, speak and act in ways that men actually like and admire. Feminists and other bitches may think they're clever or rationalize treating good men poorly in any number of ways, but they unwittingly set themselves up for disappointment, loneliness and defeat. Keepers are playing to win... and will gladly kick their flabby, entitled, selfish butts to the curb.

Keepers are rarely wilting flowers—take Sofia Vergara, Shakira, and Carrie Underwood, for example, just to name a few—but they're smart enough to know that men don't love manly, indifferent, self-centered bitches. And unlike Engle, Argov and other misguided American women, *they don't equate femininity with weakness.* They enjoy being sexy, highly feminine women and realize that respect and love from men is earned, not a birthright or unconditional entitlement.

So, if you're bending over backward to please men who don't return the favor, choosing bad boys with no hope of redemption, making excuses for jerks, or making dumb mistakes with men—like dropping all of your friends or any semblance of a life of your own—you need some new habits, but bitchiness isn't one of them. There's no need to dress, talk or act like a man, either. It's unnatural and sure to backfire.

I know that some women don't make an effort to look, talk, and act like a Keeper because they think it'll hurt more when a relationship ends if they "knocked themselves out," as Argov might say, but you can't live in fear. None of us should live that way, even if it's hard sometimes. If a man doesn't treat you with the same love and respect you show him while dating or in a relationship, you know what to do. Move on—right away. A man who's "into you" won't allow you to feel like anything other than a princess for any extended period of time. Nor should you let him. There are plenty of great guys out there looking for a girl with some self-respect, a healthy attitude, and her eye on the ball.

I gave the same tough-love advice to my younger sisters for years, and they ended up marrying really great guys. It works—even for the nice girls.

Chapter Two

Third-Wave Feminism:
Wave Goodbye to Good Men

"I would actually put [all men] in some kind of [concentration] camp where they can all drive around in quad bikes, or bicycles, or white vans. I would give them a choice of vehicles to drive around with, give them no porn, they wouldn't be able to fight—we would have wardens, of course! Women who want to see their sons or male loved ones would be able to go and visit, or take them out like a library book, and then bring them back."

— JULIE BINDEL, JOURNALIST AND RADICAL LESBIAN FEMINIST

"[Third-wave feminism] is as much a class war as it is a gender war. Much of it is perpetrated by white middle-class women who are the most privileged... group ever to have lived... waging war on working-class men... It's a sort of class hatred and class hostility perpetrated by well-fed, well-educated coastal bloggers on all the rest of us."

— MILO YIANNOPOULOS,
JOURNALIST AND DANGEROUS FAGGOT

America the Not-So Beautiful

The role of third-wave feminism in damaging gender relations in the United States and driving good men away cannot be overstated. I'm not talking about the sort of feminism dedicated to ensuring that women receive equal justice under the law. That's a worthy cause. I'm referring to the most insidious version, with its laser focus on American male-bashing at every turn. It has become mainstream and incessant over the last few decades, and it's worse now than it's ever been, especially if the guy happens to be white.

America's anti-men trend is arguably most pronounced and vicious online. In "Watch a Woman Experience 100 Instances of Street Harassment in One Day," for example, *Jezebel's* Kara Brown writes indignantly about Shoshana Roberts, who was filmed using a hidden camera as she walked along the streets of New York City for 10 hours amid catcalls, comments and other unappreciated attention from men, including one black guy who followed her around for five minutes. Brown laments that this type of "exhausting sexism" and "day-to-day bullshit... can really wear on your spirit." Indeed, according to Brown, all of this "shitty male behavior" constitutes "street harassment" that is "goddamn infuriating, frustrating and at times terrifying" and must be stopped. Here's how she so delicately puts it:

> "[T]o be clear, all of it sucks... from the innocuous, 'Hey, what's up girl,' to the man who, after she ignored a 'compliment' yelled: 'Somebody's acknowledging you for being beautiful. You should say thank you more. '*Sir, fuck your compliment and fuck your entire existence on this planet.*"

Then Brown goes on to share a truly "degrading" experience of her own while shopping at a flea market in Los Angeles. Some clown had the audacity to try to get her attention and spark a conversation by saying, "Hey beautiful." It was war. She couldn't take it anymore:

> "I quickly snapped: 'My name isn't fucking beautiful.' The man who had yelled at me came closer and said: 'I just wanted to let you know that I think you're beautiful.' I said: 'I don't give a fuck what you think.'... A few minutes later that same man approached me to apologize. He said he wasn't trying to holler at or bother me, (lies) but just wanted to give me a compliment. I told him that my self-esteem is not dependent upon the affirmation of strangers and he should stop doing that shit to me and other women."

Fortunately for the poor guy who didn't notice that big chip on Brown's shoulder, she didn't kick him in the balls, too. In "How to Kick a Guy in the Balls: An Illustrated Guide," *Jezebel's* resident ball-busting expert, Susan Schorn, recommends a swift, hard kick in the nuts for any man who puts a woman in a threatening situation. "To attack a man's testicles is to attack his identity, his virility. It also, so the rumor goes, hurts like holy hell," she says. Schorn acknowledges that it's "Pretty ugly" when it happens, but she doesn't "feel sorry for men" because "It's more than a fair trade, running the world, even if you have to keep one hand over your crotch at all times."

Now, it goes without saying that there's no excuse for truly threatening behavior toward women, including stalking Ms. Roberts for blocks on a public street like one guy did, which was way over the line. I get it, but let's be honest: Roberts walked around for *10 hours* in some dicey NYC neighborhoods in a tight t-shirt hoping that men would notice and hit on her so she could secretly film it, edit the video down to *2 minutes*, and make all men look like creeps.

I probably wouldn't have bothered speaking to a woman like Ms. Roberts in that situation, and neither would most of my friends, but that doesn't make it wrong to do so. Most of the black and Hispanic guys who did try to engage her said something complimentary or innocuous, didn't get a response, and gave up. And, while shouting "Damn!" when a hot chick walks by isn't my idea of a good opening line (especially in church), it's not an insult, and I'm sure it works once in a while. That's good enough for some guys to give it a try.

As for Ms. Brown, who happens to be black, she's an embarrassment to her gender and race. Bitter, short-tempered, foulmouthed, third-wave feminists like her tarnish the image and reputation of American women worldwide and make it harder for the best ones to receive the love, attention and respect that they otherwise deserve. They're also extremely selective in their sexist outrage. Rich, handsome guys can say "Hey beautiful" and expect to be thanked most of the time. Some even get away with conduct that would qualify as sexual harassment for the average Joe. (Google "Sexual Harassment and You" for a video demonstration.)

So I'm guessing that guy at the flea market who flirted with Ms. Brown had more than bad taste in women or poor eyesight. He was no Tom Brady... or Odell Beckham, Jr.

"I'm Not Gonna Be *Ignored!*"

As it turns out, the same feminist bitches who whine about sexism, sexual objectification, and "rape culture" when men acknowledge them for their sexual attractiveness, whine even louder when they're snubbed by men they find sexually attractive. It's confusing and maddeningly hypocritical, but it happens all the time. The latest illustration comes courtesy of one of America's most arrogant and least appealing feminists, Lena Dunham, who pounced on handsome NFL star Odell Beckham, Jr. for ignoring her at the Met Gala on May 2, 2016.

In a recent interview with fellow feminist and ostensible comedienne Amy Schumer, Dunham claimed that Beckham Jr., who sat next to her at the event, rejected her sexually by choosing to look at his cell phone rather than her, even though she went dressed as a chubby man in a tuxedo and black-rimmed glasses. Dunham put it this way:

> "I was sitting next to Odell Beckham Jr., and it was so amazing because it was like he looked at me and he determined I was not the shape of a woman by his standards. He was like, "That's a marshmallow. That's a child. That's a dog...."

> "The vibe was very much like, 'Do I want to fuck it? Is it wearing a... yep, it's wearing a tuxedo. I'm going to go back to my cell phone.' It was like we were forced to be together, and he literally was scrolling Instagram rather than have to look at a woman in a bow tie. I was like, 'this should be called the Metropolitan Museum of Getting Rejected by Athletes.'"

Dunham's fans and followers have forgiven her for all manner of sins, including a fake "Republican raped me in college" claim and a story about molesting her younger sister as a child, but "sexually objectifying" a successful black man for not paying attention to her was out of bounds, even for them. They hammered her on social media. "If you pay attention to Lena Dunham, you're sexualizing her. If you don't pay attention, you're shallow and ignoring her," wrote @MatthewKick. Precisely.

Dunham, who's as full of herself as she is full of shit, didn't simply apologize to Beckham Jr. and move on. She didn't even express regret for saying what she did about him. Instead, she tweeted an excuse: "My story about him was clearly (to me) about my own insecurities as an average-bodied woman at a table of supermodels & athletes." Then she added: 'It's my sense of humor, which has kept me alive for 30 years. It's not an assumption about who he is or an expectation of sexual attention."

That would have worked if Beckham Jr. were white, but he's not, and it didn't. So, to protect herself against the same abusive allegations of racism and sexual objectification that she hurls with glee at others for a living, she finally admitted what a neurotic, irrational schmuck she is in a rare, long-winded apology on Instagram. According to Dunham, notwithstanding her insufferable "moments of bravado," she projected her "insecurities" (about being a manly, fat, unattractive "sack of flaming garbage") on Beckham Jr., made "totally narcissistic assumptions about what he was thinking" and "presented those assumptions as facts." She also realized how unfair it was to "ascribe misogynistic thoughts" to him and contribute to a history of "over-sexualization of black male bodies" and "false accusations by white women towards black men."

I apologize if this story about Dunham gave you a headache or queasy feeling (I could barely repeat it), but here's why it matters to bitchology: Keepers don't share Dunham's crippling insecurities because they're confidently feminine and act that way by, among other things, taking good care of themselves and not showing up at big events looking, talking, and acting like a man. Keepers also don't ascribe misogynistic thoughts to men they don't know, assume that men somehow owe them their time and attention, worry about over-sexualizing men, or make false (rape) accusations towards any man, even an imaginary white Republican one.

And, unlike Ms. Brown and other man-hating feminists, a Keeper is used to attracting attention and receiving compliments from men and rarely freaks out when it happens. She expects to be noticed when she enters a room, walks down the street, or goes to the grocery store because she knows she looks good. In fact, many Keepers—especially

Latina Keepers in Miami and many parts of South America—won't even leave the house without looking like a million dollars, and they almost always appreciate it when others acknowledge their beauty in a friendly, non-threatening way.

A Keeper doesn't waste time walking around with a hidden camera looking for trouble, either. She's got more important things to do... like meeting a nice guy at the local flea market.

So, don't allow yourself to become collateral damage in the feminist war on white, working-class men and beautiful, confidently feminine women. Instead, push back against bitches who project their own insecurities and pseudo-masculinity onto you and others. They don't have your best interest at heart. They're a mess and a menace, and they need to be called out for who and what they are before even more damage is done to gender relations in the United States.

But, more importantly, live your life differently, think for yourself, and do your best to become even more of a Keeper. There aren't as many women like that in America anymore as there should be and, as the next chapter demonstrates, everybody knows it.

Chapter Three

Karma Is a Bitch

"Marriage is like a tense, unfunny version of Everybody Loves Raymond, only it doesn't last 22 minutes. It lasts forever."

— PETE (CHARACTER), KNOCKED UP (2007)

"No man is as anti-feminist as a really feminine woman."

— FRANK O'CONNOR

Yes, American Bitches Really Are That Bad

Men don't love and marry American bitches, but the troubles don't end there. They don't have sex with them either if there are Keepers around. They only end up with bitches out of desperation, a scarcity mentality, or an overall lack of self-esteem. If a good man has options and realizes it, he'll rationally gravitate away from the hostility, irrationality, and heavy, soul-sucking baggage that bitches bring with them.

In "No Sex in the City: What It's Like to Be Female and Foreign in Japan," American blogger and globetrotting feminist, Reannon Muth, opened Pandora's box by failing to understand why she couldn't get laid in Japan and taking no responsibility for it.

According to Ms. Muth, within a few weeks of her arrival in Tokyo, she was "mysteriously, frustratingly invisible." And it stayed that way for the rest of her nine-month stint as an English teacher there:

> "Most days I felt unattractive, unwanted and worst of all, unfemale. When not even a short skirt or slinky top attracted more than a passing glance and even construction workers, who could usually be counted on for a leer, regarded me with bored, blank expressions, I felt like a Martian. And very, very alone."

To make matters worse, her male expat counterparts were living like rock stars, easily hooking up with model-thin Japanese beauty queens.

Naturally, she blamed and belittled the men for not noticing, dating, and having sex with her. Japanese men "were in fact attracted to" her but were "too intimidated" to speak with "the Jennifer Anistons of the expat world." They super-secretly desired her but couldn't handle an American woman as "strong, independent, assertive and outspoken" as she was. She was "virtually un-datable" because she was just "so different, so foreign," and so *awesome*, not because no one actually wanted to date her. Meanwhile, "[d]orky," "socially awkward" expat men, also known as "White Dudes" and "white boys," were even less interested. They "flat-out ignored" her.

It didn't take long for Ms. Muth's more sensible readers to pound her with the raw, unfiltered truth: Bitchy American feminists need an attitude adjustment. Badly. Everyone knows it but them, and men won't put up with it when there are plenty of Keepers around.

Incredulous and defensive, Ms. Muth published a follow-up blog post entitled "Are North American Women Really THAT Bad?," which elicited another brutally honest response.

Here are some of the most telling comments, starting with one from a Latina who got the guy. This one really hits home:

Irene:

"I am a Colombian girl studying in the US, back in Colombia and while I lived in Europe, I was able to make many connections with women; I am straight but women were always open to me being a woman and actually trying to be friends. It's here in the USA where women according to my experience tend to be ABSOLUTELY AND TOTAL BITCHES!! Sorry but I have never been exposed to such megalomaniacs, competitive, bitchy, angry, psycho, fake, plastic women in my entire life!!!... I have NOT had a problem finding dates in America, in fact I found my fiancé here, an all American boy from Wisconsin who treat me like a princess, but guess what American women... I EARNED THAT RESPECT AND LOVE. In my country you to stay in shape, I wear dresses, skirts, make up because I ENJOY BEING A WOMAN... women here don't understand the concept of [femininity] and think [femininity] = weakness. For example I love cooking, my mom taught me to cook because it's a mother-daughter bonding thing in my culture, and guess what? I cook for me and my American boyfriend, to the point he now wants to learn how to cook... good luck finding an American girl who can cook, most of his friends dating American women just get Chinese or pizza while the slob of an American girlfriend sits there in her [pajamas] waiting for the food delivery to arrive while drinking beer... women have been nothing but evil towards me, and it's because of how I dress, of how I act, they assume I am being fake and [pretentious] but this is who I am... I can sense a deep sense of jealousy in them because they think that by me being feminine and enjoying catering to my man, I am being a fake girl! Let's not even talk about sex, American women have so many hang ups and think Sex is a tool to control men... it's pathetic but I was branded as a slut because I said I enjoy pleasing my man and being pleased by him. NO WONDER AMERICAN WOMEN OVERSEAS HAVE SUCH A DIFFICULTY FINDING MEN!"

I'm sitting in an apartment in Medellin, Colombia as I write this, and I can assure you from my experience in this country and Miami that many Latinas share Irene's view of American bitches. It obviously doesn't apply to all American women, but it does apply to the self-described alpha bitches, third-wave feminists, and social justice warriors who are urging you to join their ranks.

Tiago:

"Here in Brazil we view American women as good for sex and bad for love."

Jackie:

"If you want to see how bad [North] American women are— come sit in a divorce court. I've worked for years there and though it troubles me to admit it I have to say American women are by far the nastiest creatures I come across in my work. Half the time they just want the kids to hurt the husband and the other ha[lf] they want the money to hurt him and don't at least pretend to care about the kids. Unless women in this country stop drinking of the poison well that is man hating feminism (no I'm not talking about equal rights feminism of course) they better start learning to enjoy their cats. I see a lot of women with cats. Lots and lots of cats."

I hear Sherry Argov's next book is entitled *Why Men Love Divorce Court.*

Joe (who evidently married a "High-Maintenance Bitch"):

"I'm married to one of those ultra shallow, no good, lazy, American women. I find NOTHING good about them in general. American women are gross and unladylike. They are greedy and extremely self-centered... If I could find a way to unload this rotten bitch I'm with now and get a foreign girl, I'd do it in a second!"

divemedic:

"In my travels, I saw the same thing from a male's perspective, and I have a slightly different take on it. The problem is that American women are known the world over as being self-centered and demanding princesses who feel like men should be kissing up to their posteriors. Not so in Europe, and most assuredly not true in Japan."

Brent:

"What's been going on in the economic sector provides an excellent allegory for what's happening in the dating world right now. Western women have figuratively "priced themselves out of the market" much like what happened with organized labor in the United States and Canada. As the world is becoming more globalized, western women no longer need to fear competition from Susie down the street, but also from some other women halfway around the world. Oftentimes these women are thinner, better looking and still raised with traditional family values instilled in them. Most women overseas are happy and grateful to receive the affections of a well-educated western man from a good family… I predict that the demographic changes that will occur in the next 20 years will be astounding."

The American car industry wasn't ready for global competition and suffered greatly for it. Don't let the same thing happen to you.

Slim:

"So basically some chick goes a few months without getting laid and has to write a snarky deprecating blog entry attacking white dudes? Huh? If you can't get laid in Japan that is YOUR problem, not the fault of guys you deem to be below your standards. Rather than lashing out, your time would be better spent on improving your own negative attitude. Also, if you were really as good looking as you claim you are, I'm sure that the Japanese men wouldn't be fleeing from you like an ornery white she-[G]odzilla."

High-quality men who realize that they have options will rationally choose Keepers at home... and abroad.

Bob:

"The only reason American men date/marry American women is out of sheer ignorance. It just never occurs to most American men, living in the cocoon of American culture, that FAR better options are available. I have never met an American guy, who has dated an Asian or Eastern European lady, and then decided afterward that [he prefers] Americans. It doesn't happen. EVER. Getting away from American women is akin to finally waking up from a lifelong nightmare that you didn't realize you were in. The only hope American women have is that most American men remain insulted and ignorant of the fact that women from anywhere else on Earth are better, in every conceivable way, than their American counterparts."

George:

"Maybe some men value the sloppy-dressing, shrill, judgmental, obnoxious pseudo-men most American women have become... Your lazy, high-minded opinions on the treatment you believe to be entitled to have no value to the majority of men on planet earth. Americans are stuck with you. We are not... We (men) are just sick of being criticized & told what to do by women who haven't earned our respect. Any man who tried same would get punched in the face. But you're a woman. So we marginalize you. We ignore you. That's why we won't date you. That's why we won't marry you."

Vin:

> "I can comment on American women – particularly women in San Francisco, where I live. Friends and I joke about it a lot; the women here don't try very hard in the dating game, but expect the world from guys... I'll just use dress as one of many examples. Women in San Francisco dress like crap. They wear torn up Converse All Stars and old jeans. A hot girl can pull that off, but you have to be incredibly hot. SF women generally aren't up to that standard, and come across as lazy, entitled slobs. All you have to do is visit London, Tokyo, Seoul, Hong Kong to see the drastic differences between women—the effort they put into dating, and how they present themselves as opposed to N. American girls. I always joke with my friends that American women should be shipped off to Seoul for a couple years after college to be humbled. ha ha."

I have visited all of those cities except Tokyo (which guys rave about) and can understand why he's underwhelmed by American women in San Francisco. It's a pretty stark contrast. The same is true in Medellin and many other parts of the world.

Shane:

> "The fact is that women in North America need an attitude adjustment BADLY and the arrogance and conceit shown by "[Reannon]" are exhibit A in the case of common sense vs. the irrational and demanding white woman. She spent 2 blog entries and a total of 6-8 pages whining about how nobody wanted to put up with her nonsense overseas. SURPRISE! In a dating environment where men aren't forced to put up with rich little white girl nonsense, they

typically don't choose to put up with rich little white girl nonsense. Mind blowing stuff, I know."

Anonymous:

"The difference between the US and Europe is the way that women's rights have developed over the past 50 years and the decisions that were made to do that. In the US women saw men as having more rights and decided that they wanted to be more like men. In Europe women simply wanted to have the same rights and opportunities as men but did so without trying to take on masculine traits. This is why European women retain their femininity whereas American women see femininity as being from an era when they were treated as second-class citizens."

Excellent point. There's a big difference between wanting the same legal rights and opportunities as a man and wanting to look, talk, and act like a man.

Hmm:

"As a foreign guy, I must say that I'd never marry an American woman although they're great for some quick fun. I've seen friends marry AW and suffer through emasculation, adultery, divorce, and loss of children and worldly possessions..."

Alex:

"The value that Western women believe they possess compared to what they can actually offer a man is so out of whack, it's laughable. The men who avoided you overseas did so because for the first time in their lives, they had a choice... I blame this failing on our parents' generation more than anything else. I believe that when women won the right to get a divorce, it was intended to be used sparingly to extricate themselves from horrible situations and abusive relationships. Now it seems to be used when a women gets bored, finds a richer guy or [wants] to fleece men of half their belongings."

John:

"It's fifty million times worse for men in America. Why do you think we go abroad? Because we get treated like sh*t in our own countries unless we're mega rich or male models."

Allan:

"I have traveled all over the world conducting multi-billion dollar business, and American/Canadian women are valued about as much as a homeless man in New York City. They are viewed as feminazis, narcissistic, histrionic, materialistic, shallow, and useless... Generally speaking, American women make the worst WIVES, but are known for being great for CASUAL UNATTACHED SEX."

Andrew:

"In my years of business travels in Eastern and Central Europe, Middle East, Asia, and South America, in my years of talking with my friends who have been working and living in these countries, I have to say that it's in America where the dating rules defy all logic or evolutionary laws. In America, after graduation and college years, the dating scene is so bad, and I mean really bad, that they had to come up with online dating sites and speed dating. Really? Do men really need to fall so low, in order to find a date online or go to a speed dating event and jump from table to table every 5 minutes looking like an idiot. And at the end the chances to find a date is close to zero. I have never seen in my life where US men fell this low. It's pathetic. A man should have no difficulty to go on the street, sees a nice lady and ask her phone number and meet her later for drinks. This should be the norm and easy. But if a man with good manners, clean cut, well dressed with a good paying job regularly gets rejected, then I have to say that there is something very wrong with women in US. Something is wrong with the female mind set. And based on your article that I have read, I can see why...

However, in other countries, people don't need to go [to] online dating sites or speed dating because women are easy to approach, easy to ask out and most of the cases, they will say yes. In America it's just the opposite. Most of US women will automatically say no, like a robot, even if you are good looking, good manners and educated...

Here is the real kicker. Men from other countries are well aware of the dating situation in America. People talk. Men talk. And they are well aware of how bad US women can get when it comes to asking them out... Ladies, you don't have a good reputation at all...

Why should any guy in Japan, or Thailand or Russia or Brazil or Poland even bother to approach you when the first thing that will come out of your mouth is NO. They are not interested [in feeding] your egos."

It's true that online dating isn't necessary in many countries because men can meet women easily during their day-to-day activities, but it's taken off in many places outside of the United States anyway, including Colombia.

Energy Law:

"Honestly, it's because you American women look like livestock in high heels when surrounded by Japanese, Korean, Turkish, Polish women. And your extreme abrasive bitch personality doesn't help. So stay in those "bubbles" they call the USA or Canada. I teach English in Armenia, and your fat American white asses wouldn't get any attention here, either!"

Don't be offended by this. I"m pretty sure he's referring to Lindy West or Lena Dunham.

Randomperson:

"I personally think western women are very decadent. I blame feminism; it teaches women they are god's gift to earth and don't have to do anything to earn respect and that the world owes them everything. It teach American women that they need to be accepted for who they are and to ignore male needs. That's why 70% of American women are obese.

I'm [an] eastern European male who lives in the US, and when I go back to [E]astern Europe, the treatment I get from women is completely different. They actually respect me as a man and don't try to turn me into their personal servant.

American women on the other hand believe I owe them the world. It's actually a serious problem. The marriage rates in the US are at their lowest point. 80% of divorces are initiated by women. America's legal system is stacked against males.

I hope western women realize that their idea of equality is one sided or else western society will collapse."

I guess this guy won't be buying Sherry Argov's next book. Neither will I.

Hans:

"American women. The most entitled creatures on the planet. And even when reality takes you by the neck and shoves your noses into your sh*tty attitude you manage to blame everybody else for being nothing but horrible partners to men. You may laugh at the nerds you're feeling so much better than. But they will get laid and make money for their new families while you will end up as cat ladies when the bad-boy c*ck carousel throws you off for the new hot tweens. Karma is indeed a bitch. Love it."

To be fair, Reannon's blog posts weren't completely baseless—cultural factors surely played some part in her inability to get laid in Japan—or nearly as snide as the daily rubbish from those back-stabbing bottom-feeders at *Jezebel*. But I bet she's still in denial about the problem with American women and the opportunity it presents for Keepers at home and abroad to get and keep the best men.

By the way, as it turns out, one of my younger sisters is happily married to a fantastic Japanese-American guy, and they have two adorable kids. Yep. Some American women—the Keepers—know how to get and keep a great guy wherever they go.

The rest should think twice about claims by feminists that men love bitches. They just don't. They don't love sluts, either, for anything besides hookups and other sexual "transactions." America's best men are looking harder than ever for something and someone else.

Chapter Four

A Little Shame Goes
a Long Way

*"Miley Cyrus defended her VMA performance by
saying she made history. So did the Titanic, but only
2,000 men went down on her."*

— Joan Rivers

*"When a woman behaves like a man, why doesn't
she behave like a nice man?"*

— Edith Evans

That's a Shame

Social justice warriors, third-wave feminists, and other bitches who rail against any "shaming" of women, especially slut-shaming and fat-shaming, may be well-intentioned and make at least some promiscuous and blubbery women feel good about themselves momentarily, but they're harming those women in the long term, and they're definitely not helping you to attract, get, and keep a good man.

You have a right to be slutty, ugly, and obese if that's what you want, and I'm not suggesting otherwise. I also agree that women who love themselves are far more appealing than self-hating miscreants and malcontents who sit around and whine about their condition. But don't fool yourself about the effect your life choices are likely to have on men, chastise us for not seeing things your way, or insist that we date, love, or marry you just as you are. It doesn't work that way and never will, at least not in your lifetime.

Self-discipline is self-love, and if you aren't disciplined enough to control whom you sleep with, what you put in your mouth, when you exercise, or whether you look like a lady, you're sending the wrong signals to the men, limiting your dating prospects, neutering your sex life, and undermining your relationships.

Do you have to be perfect? Hell, no. No one is. I'm certainly not. So by all means, love yourself unconditionally–what's on the inside matters most anyway–and don't let overly negative people bring you down. But only you can improve your likelihood of success with men by making smarter choices about how you look, talk, and sleep around. No one else will care if you don't and, as explained more fully below, a little shame about poor decision-making can be incredibly helpful, if not essential, in turning things around and landing the guy of your dreams.

Slutty Is As Slutty Does

I hate to sound like a killjoy, but the cold, manly way that many American women sleep around these days has unintended consequences that are backfiring in a big way.

Since this really isn't that complicated, I'll cut to the chase:

Men lose respect for women who sleep around or have sex too quickly and easily, especially on the first date, and are less likely to love and marry them afterwards.

Guys may deny it to get laid or take advantage of you, and they are certainly part of the problem, but this book isn't about them. It's about you. What they think and do is their problem, not yours. You just need to know how to handle those men and situations in a confidently feminine way, that's all.

Many feminists and social justice warriors will tell you not to worry about acting like a promiscuous pseudo-man because riding the cock carousel somehow "empowers" or "liberates" you. They will raise the tired "double-standard" argument–if men can be promiscuous, so can you–as justification for the sluttiest behavior imaginable. Then they point the finger at men and conservative women for slut-shaming you, as if there should be no consequences for your freedom to act in self-destructive ways, and anyone who thinks otherwise is stupid or cruel.

Others simply convince themselves that sluttiness is OK—even ideal—as long as it's done right. There's actually a book called *The Ethical Slut: A Practical Guide to Polyamory, Open Relationships and Other Adventures* by "Experienced ethical sluts Dossie Easton and Janet W. Hardy." According to Amazon, customers who bought this trash also bought *Think Like a Man, Act Like a Slut*; *Why Men Love Disease-Ridden Sluts*; and *The Ethical Ho*. (Just kidding, but the books they did buy were almost as bad.)

There's even a disturbingly popular podcast entitled "Guys We Fucked: The Anti-Slut-Shaming Podcast" hosted by two snarky, repulsive American feminists, Corinne Fisher and Krystyna Hutchinson, whose parents must be mortified. Not surprisingly, they go on about how women should be able to fuck as many guys as they want, whenever they want, without shame, responsibility, or criticism. They market the podcast as comedy but, like most feminists, they're too bitchy, insecure, and over-sensitive to rise above the snark, profanity, and embarrassing anecdotes.

In a recent podcast episode, Fisher—a Jewish chick from Jersey—shared this pearl of wisdom disguised as comedic genius with her impressible female listeners:

> "There are many times in life to be shy, but my vagina is not shy... So this guy, his idea of dirty talk was to ask when was the last time I had sex with someone and I said yesterday, because it was after midnight and—it had actually been that morning—and he was not taking that well. So mid-sex, he stopped having sex with me because I have too much sex."

Fisher can invite as many guys as she wants into her gregarious vagina, and she can tell men all about it in person, on her podcast, or whenever she wants, but she shouldn't be surprised when men find it disgusting and dump her as soon as they're finished having sex, if not sooner. It's a complete turn-off. Keepers have too much self-respect to act or talk like that. Fisher and Hutchinson, on the other hand, are destined to be lonely, bitter, used-up spinsters wondering what hit them when what remains of their youth is gone.

Feminists resort to rationalizations, word games, lies, and personal attacks to avoid shame or responsibility for their promiscuity, but it rarely works when it counts. Men see right through it, especially if they've been around the block a few times. And nothing good happens in a relationship once a man loses respect for a woman, especially in the long term. The moment a guy with options realizes that you have sex at the drop of a hat with this one, that one, and the other one, he already has one foot out the door.

So, how long should you wait to have sex with a new guy? Long enough for him to have to wait a while, work for it, and prove that he's sincerely interested in you for more than sex. That time period varies depending on many factors, including how much time you spend with him each week, but most Keepers won't sleep with a guy for about a month and extend the waiting period if red flags fly in the interim.

Many women fall back on the seemingly innocuous "three-date rule" to justify banging any dude who's still standing after three dates, but it works against them for at least three reasons.

First, many gullible women figure that, since sex is right around the corner anyway, they might as well have it on the second date, first date, or even after just meeting a guy (for a one-night stand). Pressure builds not to wait for even three measly dates and just go for it... like a man.

Second, it's too easy for a jerk to send out his best representative for a few dates, tell a woman what she wants to hear, and end up in her pants. I've seen it a thousand times and often can't believe how blind women can be, perhaps willfully so. My dad once said: "You don't really know a man until you've seen him angry." Do you really know how a new guy handles his anger by the end of the third date? I doubt it.

Third and most importantly, men will be less likely to love and marry you if you're having sex on automatic pilot with every guy you date three times. If you act like sex with you is nothing special, so will he. He'll go through the motions and leave when the game is over. Robotic application of the three-date rule will get you laid, not loved and married. Is that what you want? If not, conduct more thorough due diligence on the guys you date before the main event. He'll understand.

Sherry Argov parts company with most feminists on this subject in *Why Men Love Bitches* by advising aspiring bitches to wait at least a month to have sex with a new guy. She deserves credit for discouraging promiscuity, but not for her logic.

Argov thinks relationships are about a struggle for power, not love or romance, and only encourages her readers to refrain from sex because it tilts the balance of power in their favor, or so she says. "Most men are turned on by a bitch because it's a thrill to take down a powerful woman," she says, and a smart bitch "keeps her power in *every* way." Women should act like cold, calculating bitches when it comes to sex because men perceive "an emotional woman as more of a pushover."

Wrong again, Sherry, and you just insulted millions of passionate Keepers. This isn't a tug-of-rope, business transaction, or some type of prostitution, where women essentially trade sex for money, leverage, or power over a man. We're talking about dating and relationships, where bitchiness serves no purpose. Confidently feminine women don't need to view men as the enemy or the competition to get what they want.

Privately, many Keepers will tell you (as they told me while conducting research for my other books) that American women who have sex like men are gross and embarrassing. It's practically man-on-man, they say, and it's disgusting to any self-respecting Keeper. Worse yet, this "open legs" policy has fueled a hook-up culture where horny guys think they can or should hit-it and run. That makes dating and relationships more difficult for everyone else who's looking for something more lasting and meaningful.

Keepers may look, walk, and talk sexy, and many are passionate in bed, but that doesn't mean they're acting like anything less than a confidently feminine woman when it comes to dating, sex, and relationships. They make men earn the right to be more than friends, and they give them enough time to blow it by hitting on another girl, throwing a temper tantrum, saying something stupid, not being sufficiently attentive, or otherwise not making them feel like a princess.

What about the needy guy who gestures toward his crotch with a pained expression when you pull away from some foreplay and says something like "What am I supposed to do with this?" Short answer: His blue balls aren't your problem. It's a pathetic attempt to guilt you into finishing the job that should never be taken seriously. Teasing is fair game, no matter how long it goes on without sex. Guys who think they've found a Keeper in you will wait as long as it takes.

If you're still confused about what qualifies as slutty behavior that will scare away the very guys you hope to get and keep, think of it this way: Slutty is as slutty does. There are shades of grey on the sluttiness spectrum: Not slutty, occasionally slutty, classically slutty, extremely slutty, and so on. And there's a huge difference between *acting like* a slut on rare occasions and *being* a slut all the time. Fair enough.

But here's the bottom line: Women who sleep around like men know they're sluts, at least as long as the behavior continues. So does everyone else, including the guys they "date." They're not fooling anyone in the long-term. The truth always comes out.

Yes, at least some men will date, love and marry shameless sluts–for a while at least. There's no accounting for taste, and there may be reasons for a guy to overlook a woman's repulsive sex life and long list of partners, but if you want to maximize your likelihood of landing and keeping a high-quality guy, get your brakes fixed and start pumping them–not random guys–harder and more often. Otherwise, don't be surprised when the only men who stick around are jerks and hapless beta males.

The rest of us can do better by moving on to a Keeper.

Fat Chance

Feminists and much of the media also discourage American women from losing weight in "body positivity" campaigns and accuse men who aren't attracted to beached whales of fat-shaming and bullying. They urge you to love yourself at any size and take offense if any man suggests, implies or acts as if you would be more attractive and healthier as a lighter person.

This overly simplistic position, as seductive as it is to women who are too lazy or depressed to take better care of themselves and would rather point the finger at others, works against you in several important ways.

First, Keepers who truly love themselves don't let themselves go. If they put on weight or don't look their best for some reason, they take responsible steps to improve their health and appearance and increase their likelihood of success with men. They don't play the victim or waste time blaming men for fat-shaming, bullying, or ignoring them in bars.

Second, as Milo Yiannopoulos explains in a recent article in *Breitbart* entitled "Science Proves It: Fat-Shaming Works," people who feel a sense of shame about their weight are more likely to change for the better. A study by obesity experts in 2014 showed that one of the primary factors motivating people to lose weight was a "desire to improve self-worth," especially around "life transitions" when they start worrying about social judgment and making a good first impression. Another obesity study from UCLA in 2012 actually concluded that the remedy to America's obesity epidemic lies in, wait for it... fat-shaming or, to put it more delicately, social pressure on overweight people.

Why does this matter to you? It matters because obese, man-hating feminists like Lindy West are on a crusade against fat-shaming and are encouraging other overweight and obese American women not to lose weight, with predictably disastrous consequences for their health, overall appearance, and love life.

You don't have to be an obesity expert to know that men are more likely to desire, love and marry attractive women, and an overwhelming majority of men do not find obesity attractive. Some like curves more than others, but very few are looking to date, have sex with, love or marry a woman who let's herself go. Moreover, as Milo notes in his article, there are studies showing that a man's testosterone rises just being around beautiful women, whereas obesity can lead to feelings of disgust and nausea.

Keepers don't embrace sluttiness as a lifestyle or take beauty advice from ugly feminists and other self-hating bitches. They know better than that. So should you.

Chapter Five

Bitchspotting:
Ain't That a Bitch

"One can easily conceive that in thus striving to equalize one sex with the other... one degrades them both; and that from this coarse mixture of nature's works, only weak men and disreputable women can ever emerge."

— Alexis de Tocqueville, *Democracy in America*

"In the end there is nothing more unattractive to men than radical feminism."

— Helen Fielding

Case Studies

My first book, *Field Guide to Chicks of the United States*, was about American "chickspotting," a variant of two of the world's most popular pastimes, bird watching and girl watching. My last book, *Chicaspotting: A Field Guide to Latinas of the United States*, was about "chicaspotting;" that is, the ability to find, identify, understand, and distinguish between different subcultures (or "species") of Latinas in the United States.

I didn't spend much time discussing bitches in those books because I limited their scope to observations about American women of at least marginal interest to men, but this book is different. It's a relationship guide for women who may be confused about the allure of bitchiness and the type of women whom men really love and marry.

So, in this chapter, let's take a closer look at fourteen specific subcultures of American women as case studies with an eye toward identifying conspicuous deficiencies in confidence and femininity. Then, rather than simply pointing out problems, I'll suggest remedial measures that may be helpful to you in avoiding the same mistakes, so that you can become even more of a Keeper, and get what you want from men.

The subcultures profiled below are as follows:

- The 49er (San Francisco, CA)
- The Big Sister (Third-Wave Feminist)
- The Bigger, Better Deal (Aspen, CO)
- The Boca Bitch (Boca Raton, FL)
- The Bronx Tail (New York, NY)
- The Brooding Barfly (Hipster)
- The Cougar (Sexual Predator)
- The Hole in One (Las Vegas, NV)
- The Hurt Rocker (Emo)
- The Nuyorican (Puerto Rican, Northeast)

- The Perfect 6 (Seattle, WA)
- The Sili-Clone (Orange County, CA)
- The So Ho' (New York, NY)
- The South Beeotch (Miami Beach, FL)

Each profile includes information on the distinctive appearance, voice, behavior, mating patterns, and chick magnets of that specific American subculture, along with tips—indicated by the Bitchology logo—to help you recognize and avoid bitch traps set by modern feminists. Each profile also includes a behavioral trait chart and promiscuity zipper. Here's how they work:

- **Friendliness** (with one smiley face as least friendly and five as most): Friendliness refers to how approachable and gregarious she is, how much she laughs and smiles, and how quickly she warms to strangers.

- **Neuroticism** (with one bloody cleaver as least neurotic and five as most): Neuroticism refers to how stressed out, anxious, or potentially psychotic she is or appears to be.

- **Nesting** (with one bird's nest as least interested in marriage and kids, and five as most): Nesting refers to how determined and likely she is to get married young, have kids, and settle down—but also reflects the priority that she tends to place on family, and how often she sacrifices career to be a homemaker or stay-at-home mom.

- **Maintenance** (with one hammer as lowest maintenance and five as highest): Maintenance refers to how much love, attention, or support she needs to feel satisfied in a relationship.

- **Superficiality** (with one bag of money as least superficial and five as most): Superficiality refers to how many purely superficial considerations (e.g., money, power, looks, or ethnicity) play into mate selection and serve as powerful chick magnets.

- **Promiscuity** (with one, zipped up , as least promiscuous and ten, unzipped, as most): Promiscuity refers to how likely she is to sleep around and have casual sex while single.

Now, let's go bitchpotting.

49ER™

(San Francisco, CA)

APPEARANCE: The San Francisco 49er (a "4" who thinks she's a "9"), also known as the Mission Hipster, combines styles in search of a uniquely hip, bohemian or artsy look. Funky (sun) glasses and hat, tattoos, piercings, ripped (skinny) jeans, t-shirts (with slogans), long skirts and blouses, (Birkenstock) sandals, and homemade jewelry and accessories are popular. Seldom wears fur or leather. Shaving—anywhere—is optional, as is underwear. Freeboobing is common. Normally pale, with little or no makeup or attention to her hair. Occasionally gets a short bowl cut or dreadlocks. Decent figure, but a little flabby here and there.

Shave, for goodness sake. Then strongly consider an extreme makeover to accentuate the feminine.

BEHAVIOR: Cozies up to hipsters, bohemians, and other like-minded individuals but relatively cold and unwelcoming to others, especially yuppies and prepsters. "Artistic" (broadly defined), bookish, and well-traveled. Rebellious, angst-ridden, and politically liberal but often apathetic, ideologically rigid, or nerdy. Enjoys riding her (track) bike everywhere. Likely smokes weed or uses other drugs but stays healthy with organic foods, vegetarianism, and non-traditional athletic activities.

TRAITS			
Friendliness	😀	😀	
Neuroticism			
Nesting			
Maintenance			
Superficiality			

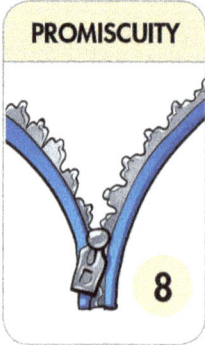

PROMISCUITY
8

THE LITMUS TEST: Active membership in the Democratic Party and associated interest groups is a trusty chick magnet in San Francisco, America's most liberal city. Any guy who's socially conservative or even moderately Republican should expect to fail the 49er's political litmus test on a regular basis.

VOICE: Highly opinionated and sarcastic but cynical, combative, and seemingly bipolar at times.

Confidently feminine women aren't grumpy and angst-ridden most of the time. So cut the groupthink and start thinking for yourself. Then lighten up, smile, and expand your circle of friends and acquaintances to include others who do the same.

MATING: Open to casual sex with a suitable partner. Often lesbian, bisexual or bi-curious, and convinced that she's hotter than she really is. Religiosity is usually a turn-off but spirituality can be an asset. Anything goes in bed because she rarely has hang-ups about sex or her body, even if she's unattractive. Known to wait for up to three dates before closing the deal.

LOWER STANDARDS AND PRACTICES: The 49er isn't prudish, but a guy should be prepared to lower his standards and take what he can get. On the bright side, he's more likely to end up in a threesome in San Francisco than most other American cities.

Have sex with anyone you like, but make him wait and work for it a lot longer. America's best men don't love or marry sluts.

MAGNETS: Normally attracted to smug hipster guys with an artsy passion project, hobby, or (if necessary) "job;" solid liberal arts education; environmental consciousness; and lots of free time to hang out. Other politically correct men who really "get" her and fit in with her friends also have a considerable edge. The rest can forget it.

BIG SISTER

(Third-Wave Feminist)

APPEARANCE: This Orwellian nightmare, also known as a feminist, intersectional feminist, feminista, social justice warrior, alpha bitch, or miserable shrew, is recognizable by a "resting bitch face" that quickly transitions into a frown with furrowed brows, a smirk, or a general look of disgust, distain, or astonishment whenever she takes offense, which happens more often than men think about sex. Typically ugly and overweight or obese, but occasionally average-looking. Rarely attractive, even if genetically blessed, once she starts trash-talking. Inclined to dress like a man, a slut, a slob, or someone who's just too lazy or busy to care. Tattoos, manspreading, and poor hygiene are common. Typically white, but an increasingly number of non-white women join the Big Sisterhood after contracting third-wave feminism like a disease from friends and the media.

NOTABLES: Lindy West, Lena Dunham, Tess Holiday, Rebel Wilson, Rosie O'Donnell, Amy Schumer, Alicia Barrón, Rachel Reichard, #TrigglyPuff, Erin Gloria Ryan, Emma Gray, Debbie Wasserman Schultz, and Hillary Rodham Clinton.

Keepers rarely settle for looking anything less than their best because it's unhealthy, unfeminine, depressing, and much harder to attract high-quality men if they do.

VOICE: Known to be shrill, loud, snarky, and humorless. (If she's laughing, it's usually *at* someone, not with them.) Lies with the greatest of ease. Condescending, even if she's talking to someone who's superior in every respect. Loves to whine, complain, and protest about alleged sexism, racism, patriarchy, homophobia, injustice, shaming, oppression, and other concepts or behavior that she deems offensive, inappropriate, or "deplorable." Habitually tries to win arguments and get what she wants by playing the victim, ignoring facts, personally attacking the opposition, and/or imposing her will. Routinely changes the plain meaning of words to suit her agenda, or just to be a pain in the ass.

BROTHER AND SISTER: In George Orwell's *1984*, the three slogans of the Party, led by Big Brother, are as follows:

War is Peace.
Freedom is Slavery.
Ignorance is Strength.

Big Sister doesn't have official Party slogans—yet—but if she did, they'd probably look something like this:

Hate is Love.
Femininity is Weakness.
Bitchiness is Confidence.

BEHAVIOR: Militant, aggressive, and prone to fits of irrational outrage over anything at any time, especially men who don't kiss her ass and Keepers who won't play her stupid, unnatural game. Normally attends or graduated from a liberal arts college that provided an indoctrination into feminist groupthink through degree studies in various forms of liberalism masquerading as gender studies, women's studies, ethnic or racial studies, or more common disciplines (especially communications, political science, and history) that have been bastardized by political correctness. Tends to work in a profession that allows her to express her grievances, especially as a blogger or some other member of the media. Occasionally tries to avoid working altogether because she hates capitalism and "patriarchy," thinks working is uncool or exploitative, or just doesn't give a shit. Normally atheistic, agnostic, "culturally" Jewish, or vaguely spiritual, with a visceral antipathy toward Christians and Christianity. Hates Islam as well but too cowardly to criticize or condemn a religion that plainly contradicts her deeply held beliefs, even when jihadists openly murder, rape, subjugate and enslave countless women around the world.

TRAITS

Friendliness	😀
Neuroticism	🔪 🔪 🔪 🔪 🔪
Nesting	🪺
Maintenance	🔨 🔨 🔨 🔨 🔨
Superficiality	💰 💰 💰 💰

PROMISCUITY

10

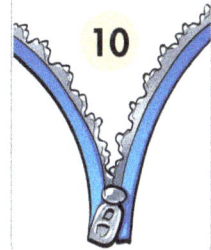

MATING: Often lesbian, bisexual, or heterosexual and desperate. Normally highly promiscuous because she sleeps around like the same male jerks who she claims to resent or despise... if she can find someone who wants to touch her. Typically hates men, especially "privileged" white, working class ones, but tolerates and encourages politically correct cowards, cucks, and beta males who kiss her ass out of fear, pity, loneliness, or lack of self-esteem. Hates beautiful women, too, especially traditional or "conservative" Keepers, who attract and marry all the high-quality men. Likely has a venereal disease, vaginal warts, and/or at least one abortion under her belt and may brag about it on social media with hashtags like #ShoutOutMyAbortion or #ShoutMyStatus. Inclined to falsely accuse men of misogyny, sexism, racism, bigotry, shaming, creepiness, sexual harassment or even rape if the opportunity presents itself. Tends to shun or postpone marriage and motherhood until it's too late to find a decent partner or her ovaries have dried up.

MAGNETS: Who cares?

Big Sister is a lost cause. It's a sad reality. She will never be a Keeper or even make a serious effort to become one because she hates beautiful, confidently feminine women, but she is potentially helpful to you as a cautionary tale, foil, or guinea pig. If you want to join the Big Sisterhood, be my guest; otherwise, let her dismal failure as an American woman be your gain. Do the opposite of whatever she does, stick with it, and you'll be even more of a Keeper in no time.

BIGGER BETTER DEAL™

(Aspen, CO)

APPEARANCE: The Bigger Better Deal (or "BBD") always puts her best face forward, even if it's barely recognizable after all the cosmetic surgery. She tends to have a large (fake) rack on a relatively slender frame, noticeably strong legs (from ski season prep exercises), optional Donald Duck lips (from collagen), and taut skin (from Botox and fillers). Wears brand-name clothing and accessories and plenty of fur.

You deserve credit for trying to look your best, and there's nothing wrong with a little surgery, but take it easy on the fake stuff, especially the duck lips. Keepers aren't interested in looking exactly like everyone else. Originality is sexy.

BEHAVIOR: Spends lots of money on fancy ski clothes. Works the après-ski circuit early and often. Well-traveled, cultured, and shrewd. Friendly and welcoming because the Aspen crowd is close-knit and exclusive but (somewhat) snobbish, pretentious, elitist, and/or spoiled. Often prefers skiing to snowboarding if she's over 30, which is usually the case.

TRAITS						PROMISCUITY
Friendliness	😃	😃	😃	😃		9
Neuroticism						
Nesting						
Maintenance						
Superficiality	💰	💰	💰	💰	💰	

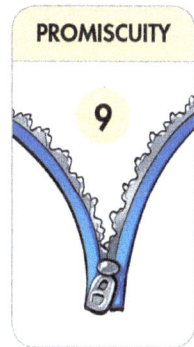

VOICE: Garrulous and opinionated, especially about shopping, vacationing, money, and the best places to see and be seen. Consummate networker and name-dropper. Always sexting because phone service is so poor. Common probing questions to sniff out the green include:

"Who do you know in Aspen?" "Where do you summer?" and "How did you get here?" (Jet-fishing)

MATING: Promiscuous, materialistic, and high maintenance. Keen on landing the most eligible bachelor and closing a bigger, better deal. Not shy about inviting a guy to her place if he hasn't made the first move. Known to wait one night to three dates before closing the deal.

HER CUP OVERFLOWETH: The high altitude in Aspen makes her a cheap drunk and easier to pick up, which explains why men routinely offer to buy drinks right away and try to keep her glass full.

MAGNETS: Attracted to guys with thick wallets and a penchant for ostentatious displays of wealth, status, or power, but any handsome guy with some animal magnetism will do. Occasionally doubles as a *Cougar*.

LISTEN TO THE MONEY TALK: The BBD will size a guy up the minute she meets him. She'll even notice which credit card he uses to pay the bill. (Black AmEx cards are like pheromones.) Regular guys can thwart the investigation and come out on top (if you will), however, by offering mysterious, open-ended answers to probing questions and refocusing the conversation on her.

Keepers may prefer men with money and power all else being equal, but they highly value non-superficial factors in men as well, don't sleep around with every rich dude who comes along, and aren't always on the lookout for a bigger, better deal.

BOCA BITCH

(Boca Raton, FL)

APPEARANCE: This borderline-tacky American woman is recognizable by straightened, fried, and highlighted or bottle-blond hair, with extensions; collagen-filled, duck-like lips with extra gloss; long claws with a French manicure; weathered skin with a spray (orangey) tan; large (fake) boobs, and a shapely body sculpted more by nip/tuck than squat/thrust. More average-looking at times. Her night-shift outfit includes high heels, trendy (mostly "True Religion") jeans or a revealing black dress, and a heavy dose of Chanel, Hermes, Louis Vuitton, and Coach merchandise. The day shift calls for plenty of Juicy Couture and big ("Jackie O") sunglasses. Normally in her mid-30s but age varies from 25 to well over 40. Often doubles as a Boca *Cougar*.

BEHAVIOR: Ostensibly wealthy because she married money (and took it in the divorce), gives it up to a rich sponsor (or series of them), or moonlights as a stripper, escort, or hooker. Drives an expensive Benz or Bentley with a big lease even though she doesn't have a real job or any money of her own. A natural-born consumer who lives to shop. Snobbish but usually poorly educated. Frequently lacks class and self-confidence but fakes it reasonably well.

TRAITS				
Friendliness	😃	😃		
Neuroticism	🔫	🔫	🔫	
Nesting	🪹	🪹		
Maintenance	🔨	🔨	🔨	🔨
Superficiality	💰	💰	💰	💰

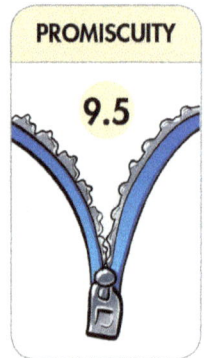

PROMISCUITY

9.5

VOICE: Shockingly profane but occasionally funny in a Howard Stern sort of way. Nosy, loudmouthed, and whiny, often with embarrassingly bad manners. Occasionally downright bossy, obnoxious, and rude.

Saunters around with an air of insouciance and a dead fish for a handshake. Reapplies lip gloss repeatedly, even at the dinner table. Chomps on gum like a cow chewing its cud. Pauses occasionally for a cigarette.

MATING: Dating, banging, fleecing, and marrying rich men—one after another—is her mission and profession. Anything else she does along the way is a means to that end. Highly competitive, territorial, opportunistic, and suspicious of other women. High-maintenance, relatively untrustworthy, and eager to upgrade. Occasionally preys on young studs for the thrill or other fringe benefits. Known to wait for one or two dates before closing the deal.

CAN'T DANCE, CAN'T SCREW: The Boca Bitch usually has no sense of rhythm on the dance floor. Count on the same performance in bed.

MAGNETS: Attracted to rich men who seem like easy prey. Frequently prefers Jewish guys, but most of them are married or uninterested. As a result, she generally ends up dating flashy, gangsterish "Guido" types and others originally from the Northeast. Non-white men have an excellent shot too as long as they're fully loaded.

BUYER BEWARE: Guys often regret getting involved with the Boca Bitch after she runs off with their shit (in a nasty divorce) or hooks up with another guy (on the side).

The Boca Bitch can only rise above her name by being a lot less materialistic, selfish, unethical, dependent, superficial, slutty, and crass. Most are lost causes, but there's hope for some.

BRONX TAIL

(African American – Northeast)

APPEARANCE: Recognizable by her slender but curvaceous bathing-suit-ready ("BSR") figure, featuring a slim waistline; (at least) medium-sized breasts; a high, shapely derriere; full hips; and lean, strong, sexy legs. Occasionally gets a boob job but usually doesn't need it. Often highly fashionable or carefully disheveled and somewhat raw. Sometimes rocks more urban attire, especially in the Bronx and Upper East Side. Regardless of whether she wears long hair extensions, a weave or goes with natural (treated) black or dark brown hair, she *owns* it. Other field marks include: Dark skin, with lighter variations; naturally full lips and strong cheekbones.

BEHAVIOR: Independent and assertive but occasionally cold, neurotic and temperamental. Often highly defensive when wearing a sexy or revealing outfit in order to clearly distinguish herself from a ho. Normally bright and ambitious, especially if she doubles as a *Bougie* (Professional African-American woman). Rarely uptight but often somewhat traditional and/or religious. Loves to dance, sing and play whenever she can.

TRAITS					
Friendliness	😀	😀			
Neuroticism	🗞	🗞	🗞	🗞	🗞
Nesting	🪹	🪹	🪹	🪹	
Maintenance	🔨	🔨	🔨	🔨	
Superficiality	💰	💰	💰		

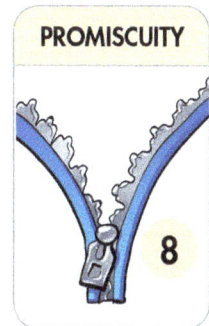

PROMISCUITY

8

VOICE: Loquacious, animated and expressive. Laughs freely and frequently. Rather loud unless well-educated. Highly opinionated and sarcastic at times.

MATING: Super-territorial, especially in her neighborhood or "borough." Stands by her man in a relationship unless he leaves her alone too long during the cold winter months. Selectively promiscuous otherwise. Relatively high-maintenance. Knows exactly what she's doing and what she wants in the sack. Waits for three dates (more or less) before closing the deal.

The bitchiness problems here are largely a function of living in New York—neuroticism and relatively high levels of maintenance and promiscuity—but there are Keepers in the Big Apple, too.

MAGNETS: Attracted to handsome, successful black men who know how to treat a lady and seem interested in a genuine relationship. Occasionally dates non-black men who are exceptionally confident, talented, and financially stable.

SURVIVAL OF THE FINEST: Non-black guys have a shot at the Bronx Tail only if they've really got their shit together and can handle a strong black chick. Others are in over their heads.

BROODING BARFLY™

(Hipster)

JOE BOVINO

APPEARANCE: This young, slender (but soft), angst-ridden chick, also known as the "PoMo" (Postmodern), strives be unconventionally attractive—with mixed results. Look for tangled, oily (dyed) hair, over-the-top tattoos and piercings, a retro pocketbook, and dark eye bags under sleepy (bloodshot) eyes. Often spotted wearing skinny jeans; wrinkled plaid shirts, vintage tops, and T-shirts; old-school sneakers; a fedora; tie; wristbands; and/or horned-rim or bug-eyed glasses. Rarely wears a bra, heels, makeup, or perfume, and occasionally has hairy and/or musky armpits. Ordinarily pale white but occasionally Asian, nerdy black, or some other ethnic variation.

THE "HAPPY HIPSTER" (PRETTY IN PLAID): Most American women who dress like a Brooding Barfly aren't the real deal. They're a Happy Hipster (also known as the "Bathing Barfly") or some other species who just wants to look cool. How can you tell the difference? If she's happy for an extended period of time, laughs and smiles a lot, and/or doesn't have a conspicuous chip on her shoulder, she's not an authentic, angst-ridden hipster.

Happy Hipsters can be Keepers because it's just a look, not an attitude, but the Brooding Barfly—while occasionally cool or attractive—tends to be a real bitch. How can she break out of it? Getting a real job and family of her own—you know, those boring traditional things—can lead to maturity and even happiness at times.

TOO COOL FOR ACTING SCHOOL: Don't confuse the Brooding Barfly with the *Mattress* (Los Angeles model/actress). Selling out and sucking up to get famous just isn't cool.

BEHAVIOR: Bar-hopping malcontent and trend-setting cool-hunter with an obscure taste in clothing, music, literature, and art. Often reasonably well-educated at a liberal arts college. Normally works as a waitress, bartender, barista, hairdresser, or retail clerk (if she's employed at all), but occasionally lands a cool job in the music, art, or fashion industries. Enjoys the late-night hipster bar scene (every day), booze and drugs, body art, reading, kids' games, organic food, smartphones, the Internet, and truly independent music. Seldom religious. Politically liberal.

TRAITS	
Friendliness	🙂
Neuroticism	🍾 🍾 🍾 🍾 🍾
Nesting	🪺
Maintenance	🔨 🔨
Superficiality	💰 💰 💰 (5 if "coolness" counts)

PROMISCUITY

9

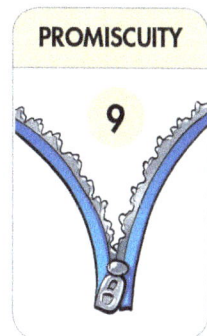

VOICE: Frequently expresses smug indifference, disdain, and/or hatred of established social norms (e.g., "work"), institutions (e.g., "Wall Street"), activities (e.g., college football), brands (except Apple), "family values," and tourists. Enjoys talking about herself (if she's in a good mood), witty banter, biting sarcasm, and self-deprecating humor. Curses like a motherf*cker. Known to brag that her vagina is "old school" (natural) and that she liked something "before it was cool."

MATING: Attracts men by acting, talking, dressing, and bathing like she doesn't care what they think. Won't hesitate to approach (hipster) guys or initiate sex, if necessary. Needs a challenge. Rarely goes on a planned "date." Tends to seek drama and instant gratification rather than love or lasting friendship, but shit happens. Known to wait one night to two months before closing the deal.

There's nothing confident or feminine about any of this. Don't act this way.

MAGNETS: Strongly attracted to narcissistic hipster guys, especially tall, skinny, pasty white ones with a bad attitude. Occasionally dates mysterious non-hipster men. Interracial dating is common.

COUGAR
(Sexual Predator)

APPEARANCE: This frisky American chick in her sexual prime (35 to 50 years old) can still turn heads. Often wears tight (loud) clothing with a padded bra, visible cleavage, lots of bling, and fuck-me pumps. Doesn't have the hard body she had in her late 20s or early 30s but stays relatively fit to attract younger men. Uses tanning, (heavy) makeup, good grooming, cosmetic wizardry, and plastic surgery—especially optional breast implants for sagging boobs—to maintain the illusion of youth. Occasionally goes way overboard.

Don't go overboard on the plastic surgery and make-up ladies, and don't shamelessly chase young men to validate yourself. Keepers grow old gracefully and have too much class and dignity to act like a Cougar or self-identify as one.

THE COUGAR FAMILY: Other members of the Cougar family include the "Puma" (under 35) and the "Sabertooth," "Snow Leopard," or "Mountain Goat" (over 50, menopause, dentures).

BEHAVIOR: A seasoned MILF, divorcee, widow, or childless career-oriented woman on the biological clock. Tends to be smart, financially successful (one way or another), and goal-oriented. Ostensibly confident (in some ways), dominant, and determined to get her way. Occasionally jaded and cynical about men, especially older ones.

TRAITS				
Friendliness	😀	😀	😀	
Neuroticism	🍾	🍾	🍾	
Nesting	🪺	🪺		
Maintenance	🔨			
Superficiality	💰	💰	💰	💰

PROMISCUITY
10

Cougars are aging, pathetic sluts. Men don't love or marry sluts, at least not on purpose.

VOICE: Doesn't hesitate to talk dirty, in or out of bed, or cut to the chase. Lies about her age if necessary.

MATING: A stalk-and-ambush predator who preys on much younger men. Sly, smooth, seductive, and cunning as she goes for the kill. Often prefers to be the aggressor and enjoys role reversal. Non-committal as she moves from one younger mate to the next. Usually has a been-there-done-that attitude toward marriage. Rarely plays the head games that younger American women do and knows exactly what she's doing in bed. Closes the deal early and often… if she can.

HOT FOR TEACHER: She may be a little old and wrinkly, and her relationships with younger men may have no long-term potential whatsoever, but she's a seasoned slut who can teach disposable boy-toys a thing or two in and out of the bedroom.

MAGNETS: Attracted to guys in their 20s or early 30s with no beer belly, a full head of hair, and an overactive libido to match her own. Expands the net in her 40s and 50s to include men in their mid to late 30s.

HOLE IN ONE™

(Las Vegas, NV)

APPEARANCE: There are lots of fat women in the buffet lines at Las Vegas casinos, but the Hole in One isn't one of them. She tends to be slender or athletic and toned, with a provocative outfit, plenty of makeup, and a devilish gleam in her eye. Occasionally more average looking, but always dressed to impress and attract attention.

HOLE IN ONE LIGHT: An American woman who resides in Vegas but isn't selling sex (in one way or another) is a *"Hole in One Lite."* She tends to be much less complicated and more laid-back than the Hole in One, with a casual, Western style; been-there-done-that attitude; and a preference for heavy drinking in local dive bars over the Strip. She also tends to be more relationship-oriented but relatively kinky and/or open-minded about "swinging," threesomes, and other unconventional sexual activities.

HO SPOTTING: A conspicuous minority of Hole in One's are hookers. How can you spot them? If a Hole in One is attractive, scantily clad, and way too easy for an average guy to meet and pick up, chances are she's a ho, especially if she initiates the conversation with him, appears to be alone, and seems a little too familiar with the bar staff. Use your common sense. The Hole in One is promiscuous but rarely a sure-thing unless she's workin' hard for the money.

BEHAVIOR: Amped up and ready to party with a smile and a bounce in her step. Lives for the moment and seeks instant gratification through dancing, drinking, gambling, and sex (with strangers). Also enjoys the shows, concerts, strip clubs and big events, especially on vacation. Often smokes (after a few drinks) or uses recreational drugs.

TRAITS					PROMISCUITY
Friendliness	😀	😀	😀	😀	10
Neuroticism					
Nesting					
Maintenance					
Superficiality					

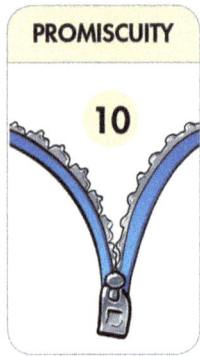

VOICE: Common expressions include: "I've never done this before!" "Oh my God!" "Do you have a condom?" and "I'm so fucked up."

Slutty is as slutty does, and this is as manly and insecurely promiscuous as it gets. Keepers know that going to Vegas doesn't mean they have to have sex with a complete stranger. They think for themselves and make their own decisions about what's best under the circumstances, especially if they're already in a relationship.

MATING: Highly promiscuous and sexually aggressive, even if a guy seems to be taken. Pursues and engages in sexual activity like a man, even if she ordinarily wouldn't act that way someplace else. Normally harmless and carefree but occasionally psycho. Complicated only if a guy cares to see her again after a night or two. Known to wait one night to three "dates" before closing the deal.

SHE HAPPENS IN VEGAS: If a guy wants a one-night stand, lap dance, or some pricey "company," he's in luck. If he's looking for love or a serious relationship, his odds are better at the slot machines.

MAGNETS: Strongly attracted to wealthy men and sugar daddies who subsidize her wild side. Also drawn to boy-toys looking for some action with no strings attached.

HOW MUCH?: Relatively handsome guys with disposable income have what it takes. Their job is to pay for drinks, dinner, drugs, or maybe just an hour of her time.

Keepers aren't off-the-charts superficial, even in Vegas.

HURT ROCKER™

(Emo)

APPEARANCE: This emotional, oddly sexy chick, also known as the "Finding Emo," is recognizable by her sour expression; pasty white skin; jet-black short or shoulder-length hair with sharp edges and shapes, usually with (flamboyantly highlighted) bangs covering at least one eye or sections pulled in different directions (and dyed blond at times); thick eyeliner; dark or bright red lips; ridiculously tight jeans; tight, short-sleeved (black or dark colored) T-shirts with the name of her favorite band on them; and beat-up, old-school sneakers. Her (borderline) trashy or slutty outfit also includes (white) studded belts, wristbands and armbands (with bright colors), bright-colored jewelry (with skulls and crossbones), band merchandise, and optional black-rimmed glasses. Piercings are common, especially lip and nipple rings.

EMO, GOTH, OR PUNK?: Try not to confuse the Hurt Rocker with even gloomier Goth chicks or irreverent punk rockers who also tend to wear black clothing and dark makeup on pasty white skin like it's Halloween every day. Hurt Rocker puts a lot of time and energy into her distinctive "emo" style and expects you to notice the difference.

BEHAVIOR: Either suffers from bipolar disorder or acts like she does. Relatively shy, sullen, anti-social, and mysterious, even though she's usually from a comfortable, middle-class family. Tends to avoid eye contact with strangers. Highly sensitive, pessimistic, and cynical. May actually cut her wrists (and cover them with wristbands) if she's really screwed up. Often vegetarian. Loves emo, indie, and underground music; plus "deep" poetry, "art," and taking pictures or video of herself from strange angles to post on emo websites.

SUBCULTURE	COMMON NAME
HURT ROCKER	EMO

TRAITS

Friendliness	😃
Neuroticism	(five icons)
Nesting	(two icons)
Maintenance	(four hammers) *(emotional)*
Superficiality	(three money bags)

PROMISCUITY

9

(Unless "sXe")

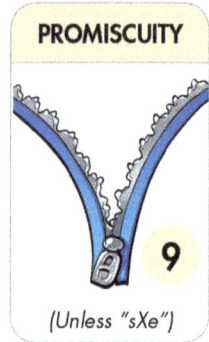

If you have to be Emo, let's hope it's just a phase. The sooner it ends, the better.

VOICE: Vacillates wildly from introverted brooding to emotional outbursts at inappropriate times. Cries and curses frequently.

LET HER VENT: If a guy can't handle a little venting and profanity from the Hurt Rocker, he's not the man for the job. She's going to emote. That's who she is.

MATING: Loves to kiss emo guys, watch emo guys kiss, or kiss another Hurt Rocker. (It's hard to tell them apart.) Typically views sex as a way to boost her poor self-esteem, express her emotions, and feel loved or accepted by others, at least until she matures. Occasionally adopts a "sXe" lifestyle (pronounced "straight edge") and refuses to drink, smoke, masturbate, or have sex. Known to wait one night to three dates before closing the deal (unless sXe).

MAGNETS: Strongly attracted to male emos with similar tastes, interests, and antisocial tendencies. Occasionally dates other guys, especially if they're highly sensitive, emotionally troubled, or there's chemistry for some other reason. Normally avoids posers, jerks, and insensitive players.

NUYORICAN
(Puerto Rican – Northeast)

APPEARANCE: The Nuyorican [noo-yor-ree-kan], also known as the "Ledge" or the "Shelf," tends to have an urban or ghetto-urban style due to extensive intermingling of Latin and black cultures in the region, but she glams it up at times. Look for a big, protruding butt, with naturally small to medium-sized breasts, golden brown skin, a prominent forehead, beautiful brown eyes, and long, dark brown hair. Often petite to medium-height. Breast implants are not the norm but increasingly common.

TWO POTATOES ON STICKS: Jennifer Lopez is America's most famous Nuyorican. She put it this way: "As a Latin woman in the United States, you're taught that you should be skinnier, that you shouldn't have such a big butt. You feel self-conscious. I did. I was really thin, but I had a booty on me that you would not believe, like two potatoes on sticks." There was, however, a fringe benefit: "I could serve coffee using my rear as a ledge."

NOTABLES: Rosie Perez, Jennifer Lopez, Jessica Caban (model girlfriend of Bruno Mars), LaLa Anthony, Talisa Soto, Adrienne Bailon (1/2 Ecuadorable), and Rosario Dawson (1/2 NYC So Ho'), and Raquel Reichard (book-banning feminista).

BEHAVIOR: Family-oriented and spirited but not particularly friendly to strangers and occasionally (somewhat) aggressive. Often relatively uneducated and poor—with a poverty rate similar to the African-American *Bronx Tail*—but animated and passionate about life. Usually loves urban and Latin music (including lots of reggaeton), watching the "novelas," dancing, and singing.

TRAITS

TRAITS					
Friendliness	😃	😃			
Neuroticism	🔪	🔪	🔪	🔪	🔪
Nesting	🪺	🪺	🪺	🪺	
Maintenance	🔨	🔨	🔨		
Superficiality	💰	💰			

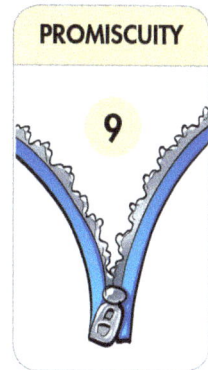

PROMISCUITY

9

DUAL IDENTITY: The Nuyorican has a dual identity (crisis) because she shares cultural traits with fully assimilated American blacks in the Northeast that differ greatly from the *La Guitarra* in South Florida and Puerto Rico.

VOICE: Talks quickly and loudly. Tends to curse, use urban slang, say "culo" (ass) and "Que carajo!" (What the fuck!), mangle grammar, and gesture dramatically. Often refers to her man affectionately as "papi" (daddy) or "chulo" (cutie) unless she's upset with him, in which case he's a "pendejo" (dumbass) or "sangano" (idiot). Frequently speaks English (or Spanglish) rather than Spanish but conversant in both languages.

MATING: Fickle, sexy, and promiscuous while single, but extremely territorial in any exclusive relationship. Tends to have a non-traditional family structure and stay single longer than most other Latin American species. If she has a child out of wedlock—as often happens—she'll go after the biological father for child support until she gets it or they repo his ride. Known to wait one night to two weeks before closing the deal.

Most Nuyoricans are proud, free-thinking Latinas, but too many pick up the insecurities and manliness of their white and black friends in the Northeast who poison their minds with third-wave feminism. It happens to *Beauty Calls* (Dominican-American women) in the region as well. These "feministas" are some of the most hyper-sensitive, irrational and iron-fisted feminists in the country, and they're easy to find in the media, especially online.

MAGNETS: Attracted mainly to Latin and black guys, especially bad boys and players. Occasionally dates other types with a compatibly urban lifestyle and worldview.

PERFECT 6™
(Seattle, WA)

APPEARANCE: This earthy chick is rarely hotter than a 6 but harder to pick up than a 10 in many other American cities. Usually has an average body with smooth, pale skin (from all the rain) but pays less attention to hair, makeup, and personal grooming than most American women, resulting in noticeably hairy body parts on the proud "granola" or hippie version. Inclined to wear fleece sweaters, T-shirts, jeans, Birkenstocks (with socks), a Gore-Tex storm jacket, and other stuff from North Face, Lands' End, REI, or Eddie Bauer. The end result tends to be bland, nondescript, or unkempt.

CHICK OR DUDE?: The Perfect 6 looks eerily similar to the male equivalent, making it difficult to distinguish between them at times. This is especially true if she doubles as a *Hurt Rocker* from the thriving "emo" (emotional) and indie music scene in Seattle.

Keepers are never mistaken for men, even in high-powered professional jobs. You can dress for business and inclement weather without hiding your femininity completely.

BEHAVIOR: Introverted, socially awkward, and relatively unwelcoming. Normally well-read, highly educated, and progressive but coolly aloof, cliquish, and class-conscious. Also tends to be noticeably edgy, whiny, or melancholy because of all the gloomy weather. Enjoys neighborhood cafes and outdoor activities (e.g., camping, kayaking), weather-permitting. Often politically liberal and non-religious.

TRAITS					PROMISCUITY
Friendliness	😃	😃			
Neuroticism	🍾	🍾	🍾		
Nesting	🪺	🪺			**7**
Maintenance	🔨	🔨	🔨		
Superficiality	💰	💰	💰	💰	

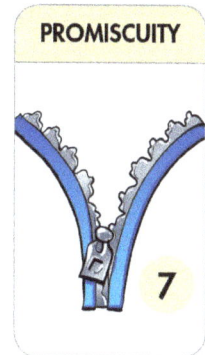

THE SEATTLE FREEZE: Guys who aren't from the Northwest tend to get a frosty reception—known as the "Seattle freeze"—because the Perfect 6 is even colder when it comes to outsiders.

> Stop acting like a cold bitch, especially with people from out of town. It's unappealing on so many levels. Keepers are sweet and friendly without being pushovers.

VOICE: Chatty online. Offline... not so much. Sticks to the keyboard because Seattle has a high percentage of online daters. That's where the action is—in cyberspace.

MATING: All those cute coffee shops don't translate into much sexual energy because the Perfect 6 is rarely flirtatious, relatively serious, and extremely picky. The degree of difficulty increases even further if she's bi-curious, lesbian, or angry at men in general for some reason. Known to wait for three dates before closing the deal.

> You're picky without making much of an effort to attract men because you think you can get away with it in Seattle. That's probably not true, and you better not move because that attitude ain't gonna fly in most other parts of the country.

MAGNETS: Attracted to wealthy local (tech) guys who know how to chill out and spend money on average-looking American women. Also drawn to "real" men, rugged outdoorsmen, and successful artists who have something interesting to say and aren't holding out for Jessica Simpson. Unlikely to judge or hassle guys who smoke, drink beer, or do drugs because she probably does (or has) too.

SILI-CLONE™

(Orange County, CA)

SUBCULTURE	COMMON NAME
SILI-CLONE	ORANGE COUNTY, CA

APPEARANCE: Cross between Malibu Barbie and Jenna Jameson. Tends to have straight, fried (platinum) blond hair; an orangey tan; huge, rock-hard fake boobs; and a shapely, tight butt. Often size 2 or less and relatively fit. Other field marks include fake nails; swollen lips; lots of makeup; a big wedding ring on the wrong finger; a flashy, studded-out designer outfit—pink is a popular color—or revealing top and jeans; expensive shoes; and the trendiest brand-name accessories.

BEHAVIOR: Saccharine sweet and sociable but conniving, pretentious, and pampered. Nonchalant and convivial but insecure, unstable, and needy at times. Normally somewhat socially conservative and ostensibly religious. Often supports her carefree lifestyle with cash from rich parents, a sugar daddy, or large alimony and child support payments. Loves to sunbathe, go boating, socialize, and shop.

TRAITS						PROMISCUITY
Friendliness	😁	😁	😁			
Neuroticism	🔪	🔪	🔪	🔪		
Nesting	🪺	🪺	🪺			
Maintenance	🔨	🔨	🔨	🔨	🔨	
Superficiality	💰	💰	💰	💰	💰	7

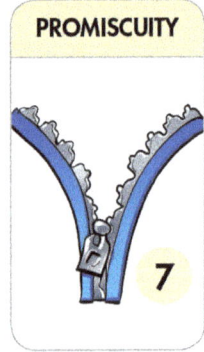

Confidently feminine women don't need a sugar daddy or rich ex-husband to be happy and successful. Make your own way and choose a mate for other, less superficial reasons.

VOICE: Laughs too hard at corny jokes by wealthy guys, especially if she's young. Highly catty and gossipy. Common expressions include: "She's so 909." (Translation: That skank lives in a less affluent county covered by the 909 area code, such as far eastern LA County, southeastern San Bernardino County, or portions of Riverside County).

Keepers strive to look sexy and beautiful without crossing the line and resembling a porn star. Guys ogle and have sex with porn stars; they rarely love or marry them.

MATING: High-maintenance gold digger (in her sexual prime) who competes fiercely against other Sili-Clones. Too conservative and image conscious to be overtly promiscuous or slutty—before a few lavish dates anyway—but horny and not above using sex to reel-in a good catch. Craves attention, photo ops, and social networking "friends." Often resorts to desperate measures or doubles as a *Cougar* by her mid-30s. Known to wait for up to three dates before closing the deal.

BATTLE OF THE CLONES: Young Sili-Clones in their 20s and early 30s shamelessly hang out with wealthy lizards in their 50s and 60s, especially if the economy is bad. Older Sili-Clones are seriously interested in these ballers too and hot enough to compete for them after a little nip/tuck.

Most decent guys hate it when women try to develop a serious relationship by trading sex for money. It's borderline prostitution. (At least real prostitutes are honest about it.) Keepers don't sell themselves and land higher quality men as a result.

MAGNETS: Strongly attracted to ostensibly rich white guys in their 30s to 60s, even if they're otherwise unattractive or sleazy. Occasionally dates non-white men if they're equally loaded and generous. Hooks up casually with other types every now and then because she can only go so long without sex. Ridiculously starstruck when celebrities venture behind the Orange Curtain (i.e., the border of Orange County, CA).

SO HO'

(New York, NY)

APPEARANCE: This cosmopolitan woman tends to be slender from all the walking around but a bit soft and pale because the weather and fast pace of New York take their toll. Doesn't hesitate to wear unflatteringly casual clothes (e.g., tank top, sweat pants) with little or no makeup for day-to-day errands but tends to be super-trendy, chic, and highly accessorized for work, special events, or a night on the town, with a nice designer jacket and handbag. Occasionally opts for a cooler, more bohemian look if she's artsy, proudly European, or showers less frequently for some other reason. Black is a popular color. Open to cosmetic and plastic surgery—it beats working out and saves time—but not as obsessed with her appearance or the opinions of others as many other American women.

Making little or no effort to dress well, look great, and smell good for much (if not all) of the day isn't how Keepers roll. Fortunately, this problem is easy to solve if you're motivated to do so, and some So Ho's and So Ho Mo's already look pretty damn good.

THE SO HO' MO: The So Ho' model (aka the "So Ho' Mo") is notorious for spending hours in front of a mirror to create the illusion that she's gorgeous even when (meticulously) disheveled.

BEHAVIOR: Smart, worldly, and doing just fine without a steady guy (or so she tells herself). Culturally open-minded and tolerant but noticeably cold, jaded, defensive, or bitchy at times, especially around strangers. Often tenacious, intense, and aggressive in pursuit of her goals. Works and plays hard but periodically feels stressed-out and overwhelmed. Tends to be (somewhat) politically liberal or libertarian and relatively non-religious.

SUBCULTURE	COMMON NAME
SO HO'	NEW YORK, NY

TRAITS	
Friendliness	😄
Neuroticism	🍾 🍾 🍾 🍾 🍾
Nesting	🪺
Maintenance	🔨 🔨 🔨 🔨 🔨
Superficiality	💰 💰 💰 💰

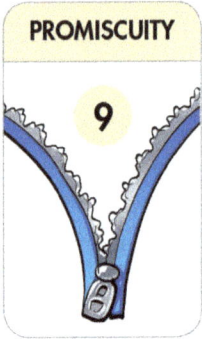

PROMISCUITY

9

VOICE: Highly opinionated, direct, and brutally honest, especially about a guy's shortcomings. Talks loudly and quickly but normally has something (at least marginally) interesting or amusing to say. Often witty and sarcastic, albeit crude, snarky, and condescending at times. Won't hesitate to call a guy out if he acts like a jerk, idiot, racist, or misogynist, which he's bound to do on a regular basis because she redefines those words at will to get her way.

MATING: Highly promiscuous, fickle, and wary of men in general, as glamorized by the "Sex & The City" television show and movies. Open to the occasional one-night stand or casual fling. Tends to have sex like a man—quickly, detached, or even just to relieve stress—but there's usually a softie (way) behind the tough-chick act. Typically far more concerned about her own needs and pleasure than her partner's, even if she won't admit it. Takes the initiative in courtship and chases the men she really wants, if necessary.

"Sex & The City" was a well-written, highly entertaining show, but none of the main characters were Keepers, especially the two sluttier ones. Carrie and Mr. Big got married in the end, but only because the show needed a happy ending. In real life, he marries a Keeper instead.

MAGNETS: Attracted to guys of almost any ethnicity or race who can keep up with her, satisfy her every need, and respect her independence. She wants it all—intelligence, humor, looks, money, and great sex—but usually settles for less because the competition for great guys in New York City is stiff.

SOUTH BEEOTCH™

(Miami Beach, FL)

APPEARANCE: (Overly) tan and slender or athletic and toned. Often installs a rack (breast implants) if her boobs aren't naturally big but may not bother if she's already smoking hot or thinks she is. Sunbathes in a skimpy bikini (occasionally topless) and hangs out in oversized designer sunglasses, flip-flops, and as little clothing as possible. Hits the clubs at night in outrageously sexy outfits designed to make men drool.

BEHAVIOR: Lives for the next day at the beach and the party afterwards but not particularly friendly or approachable unless you're on the same program and in her league. Rarely bright, well-educated or religious because it interferes with having a good time. Tends to drink like a fish (at your expense) but dances and exercises so much that it doesn't show. Frequently uses drugs like ecstasy and cocaine to party late into the night and early morning.

TRAITS					
Friendliness	😁	😁			
Neuroticism	🔪	🔪	🔪	🔪	
Nesting	🪺				
Maintenance	🔨	🔨			
Superficiality	💰	💰	💰	💰	💰

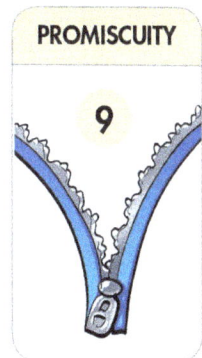

PROMISCUITY
9

VOICE: Specializes in the booty call, booty text, and sext. Anything else she has to say in clubs is drowned out by the music, but it hardly matters. It's all small talk. Most of what she wants to say is conveyed in body language.

MATING: Shamelessly promiscuous. Performs an elaborate courtship dance in response to trendy house music. Alcohol and drugs grease the wheels for guys willing to play along, where sex often happens at 4 or 5 a.m. on a weeknight in exchange for the freebies. Often open-minded and enthusiastic about sex with other women—the real deal or just enough to tease men— or multiple partners. Occasionally parties too hard and ends up sloppy drunk, high, or saddled with a venereal disease. Capable of detaching intimacy from sex and "dating" several guys at the same time. Known to wait one night to three "dates" before closing the deal.

There's nothing wrong with dancing, drinking, having fun, and meeting guys in the bars and lounges of South Beach, but Keepers just aren't this slutty. Men don't love or marry pseudo-prostitutes—at least not for long—no matter how sexy and beautiful they are. So don't overdo it.

MAGNETS: Attracted to guys with something to trade for sex, such as VIP treatment at the best clubs and private parties, an impressive boat, fancy car, big house or condo, or free drinks, drugs, and dinners. Good looks go a long way, too.

If you wouldn't be with a guy without his money, you're trading sex for that money to some extent. Reconsider.

Chapter Six

The Keeper Principles

"Success leaves clues."

— TONY ROBBINS

"You better work, bitch."

— BRITNEY SPEARS, *WORK BITCH*

Becoming more of a Keeper isn't as easy as it sounds. The same goes for guys who strive to become more confidently masculine. It takes time to develop new and improved habits that increase the likelihood of success in dating, relationships, and life in general, but it's doable, and the effort required is always worth it.

This chapter will expand upon remedial measures suggested in previous chapters by setting forth 15 "Keeper Principles" designed to do only one thing: help you do an even better job of turning the heads and winning the hearts of America's best men. That's why I wrote this book.

So, without further ado, here are the Keeper Principles:

Keeper Principle #1
Count Your Blessings
(Stop Bitching about What You Lack)

You can't improve your life or your luck with men until you improve your mindset and attitude. It all starts on the inside. Good things rarely happen to people who walk around looking at their shoes with a frown on their face, a chip on their shoulder, and a snide comment on the tip of their tongue.

So, before you do anything else, take a minute or two each day to count your blessings. Thank Jesus, God, your Higher Power, your best friend, or the dog—whatever works for you. You can even thank me if you want to, but I prefer expensive gifts. If you're alive and kicking, you have plenty to be grateful for, especially if you were lucky enough to be born in the United States. Keepers know how blessed they are, and it shows.

There are plenty of studies demonstrating that the key to happiness is gratitude. That should be reason enough to cultivate a habit of thankfulness, but there's another huge benefit: Men love it, especially when you're happy for reasons having nothing to do with the relationship. Why? Besides the obvious benefits of hanging around a cheerful woman, men don't feel pressure to make you happy. Only you can make yourself happy for any extended period of time. A great relationship can improve and enrich your life in meaningful ways, but your happiness is up to you.

Nobody likes an ingrate, especially a bitchy one. Strive to be a grateful, happy Keeper instead. Good men naturally gravitate to women like that.

Keeper Principle #2:
Get Lucky with Men by Capitalizing on Mystical Coincidences (Don't Force It or Push Too Hard)

You can do your best to look, talk and act like a Keeper and put yourself in a position to succeed with men, but you can't make things go your way by sheer force of will. No matter how hard you try or how determined you are to attract, get and keep a great man, many things will be out of your control.

So you have a choice. You can try to force it, put a lot of pressure on yourself, and end up frustrated, or you can let the universe do its part— or let God do His—by paying close attention to the messages that you receive in the form of mystical coincidences and capitalizing on them.

It's a joint enterprise: If you allow the energy of your soul to connect and work with the energy of the universe, nature, or God, you'll be more likely to succeed in every aspect of your life, including dating and relationships. Of course, you can't rely on God or anything else to do *all* of the heavy lifting. If you sit at home and wait for your luck to change, nothing is going to happen. You need to get out there and mix it up, but you can't do it all by yourself because so much is out of your control. So, look for meaning and divine guidance in coincidences that occur while you're doing your thing.

I realize that it's often hard to distinguish a mystical coincidence from a meaningless one. Sometimes, if you're paying attention, you can *feel* the universe or God speaking to you when something happens, like an old friend calling or texting you out of the blue when you were just thinking about them, an opportunity that arises just when you need one, or even a book (like this one) that calls you to action in a certain way. Other times, you'll wonder about the significance of a specific coincidence—I certainly do—but that's where your instincts and intuition come into play.

If you're still stuck or want to tap into the energy of the universe or God in a more direct way, just come out and ask for a little divine guidance. If you don't know how to ask or what to do or say, try this simple prayer: *"Show me the way."* That's it—4 short words. You may not have an epiphany or get your answers right away, but you'll be looking a little more closely for those mystical coincidences, and you never know what they'll be. One of them may even materialize in the form of a really great guy. I hope so.

Keeper Principle #3:
Think for Yourself.
(Reject Feminist Groupthink)

Do you really need feminist rags like *Jezebel*, *Huff Post Women*, and *Latina Magazine*, or feminist books like *Why Men Love Bitches, Shrill* or *The Ethical Slut* to tell you what to think and believe about men? No, you don't. You may enjoy the comradery and social acceptance that feminist groupthink brings, but you'll never be a Keeper if you don't learn to think for yourself, even if it means butting heads with aggressive, closed-minded women who don't appreciate your intellectual independence.

Educate yourself and consider different· points of view before reaching a conclusion about things–especially bitchiness and men. Don't allow feminists to indoctrinate you with hateful propaganda, redefine the plain meaning of words, ignore facts, or persuade you to look, talk, and act like someone you're not–a bitch, a man, a walrus, whatever. And, by the same token, don't make excuses for men who treat you like anything other than a princess. Dump them too. You can do better than that.

The raw, unfiltered truth is simple, manageable, and right there in front of you if you choose to acknowledge and act on it.

Let's stick with that, shall we? Yes, we can!

Keeper Principle #4: Look like a Beautiful, Confidently Feminine Woman (Don't Look Like a Man)

Keepers often go to extraordinary lengths to look like a million bucks every time they leave the house, and they usually look damn good inside the house too. I don't know how they pull it off, but they obviously attend meticulously to their hair, makeup, clothing, and accessories; proudly show off their best assets, even if they're overweight. They work out regularly and watch what they eat. And, if necessary, they take advantage of cosmetic and plastic surgery. Whatever it takes.

They do it because it makes them happy to look sexy and feminine, not out of weakness, and they enjoy doing things that please men. They feel more confident and empowered when they look beautiful, and it shows. Feminist bitches and other women who follow their lead often look like pseudo-men, sluts or slobs by comparison. It's relationship suicide.

Guys are visual. We may be simple, but we're not stupid, and we have a choice. We love women who make an effort to look like a beautiful woman, not a man, and do the best they can with what God gave them.

So step it up, ladies. Not all of you. You know who you are.

Supermodels and other smoking-hot women can get away with baggy sweatpants, oversized t-shirts, bad hair, no shower, and no makeup in public. The rest of you can't, especially if you don't have a great body. That's why Keepers rarely let their guard down and run around town looking like a bum. You shouldn't either—at least not on a regular basis—if you want to attract, get and keep a great guy.

Keeper Principle #5:
Copy the Keepers
(Don't Copy Feminists or Men)

Tony Robbins knows a thing or two about motivating people to improve their lives, and he's right about a fundamental, overarching principle for achieving success in attracting, getting and keeping a great guy and anything else that matters to you: *"To be successful, find someone who's achieved the results you want and copy what they do."*

Think about it. Have "Alpha Bitch" Gigi Engle, Kara Brown (*Jezebel's* resident flea-market shrew), Lena Dunham, or any other modern feminist really achieved the results you want with men? They're a fucking mess, unless you define success as making yourself repugnant to most people and attracting male leftovers. Keepers, on the other hand, are succeeding with men in ways that can work for you right away if you pay attention and copy what they do.

So study the Keepers, especially the ones who you admire the most. Then copy them. Not everything they do. Just the stuff that works with men. There's no way you won't improve your life and luck with men if you're patient and stick with it.

Keeper Principle #6:
Accentuate Your Natural, God-Given Femininity
(Stop Trying to Be a Man or Alpha Bitch)

Keepers *like* being womanly, sexy, seductive, and highly feminine. It comes naturally, and they're not interested in faking it. It doesn't matter whether they're poor and financially dependent or wealthy and well-educated with a successful career of their own. Either way, *they don't want to be masculine or act like men.* They expect actual men to do that.

Needless to say, guys love it. You can find exceptions to the rule who seemingly prefer their women to wear the pants in a relationship, but do you really want to carry some loser's balls around in your purse? If so, be my guest. Marry a beta male, a pussy, or a gay man who needs a beard, but you're settling, and you know it, and it doesn't have to be that way.

Some American women get it, particularly in Texas, other southern States, and many parts of the Midwest. They don't need anyone to remind them to be proudly feminine.

Many Asian, Latin, Middle Eastern, and European women also view femininity in a far more positive light than American feminists. One of them, British-Lebanese Amal Alamuddin, even convinced George Clooney to tie the knot. Another, Chinese-Vietnamese-American Priscilla Chan, wed billionaire Facebook CEO Mark Zuckerberg. I don't know Mses. Clooney or Zuckerberg, but Lebanese-American women—90% of whom are Christian—"tend to be feminine but rarely a feminist" and "loyal to [their] huge, well-connected family, especially the elders," to quote my first book. Likewise, Chinese-American women tend to be "independent but family-oriented and raised to nurture and please [their] man." Men really like these things.

Not surprisingly, American feminists have tried to spin these celebrity marriages to their advantage. One blogger for *Huff Post Women*, Kristen Houghton, actually claims that these nuptials changed the meaning of "trophy wife." Before Clooney and Zuckerberg tied the knot, American men preferred a "docile" woman who would act as a "servant" and "brainless beauty on [their] arm at social functions..." But now, she says, "Brains are the new beauty" and "the most attractive and sexually desirable women" are "alpha" bitches who aren't "afraid to *intimidate* any male that has antiquated ideas of gender roles." (My italics) We should all rejoice in the "rise of the alpha woman" and exclaim, "Hooray equality!"

Not so fast.

Houghton's article is misleading—deliberately so—for three reasons. First, Clooney married a *foreigner*—not an American feminist—and Zuckerberg married a woman who, while born in the United States, appears to identify with the Chinese culture and/or Confucianism. Neither one fits the description of an American "bitch" or third-wave feminist. Second, if brains are the new beauty and looks aren't all that important anymore, why did Clooney, in particular, choose to marry such a hottie? Third, Houghton and her ilk are so obsessed with being "strong," gaining "power," and becoming an "alpha" bitch that they undermine the appeal of femininity by associating it with weakness. There's nothing more formidable than a confidently feminine Keeper who isn't trying to intimidate men or, worse yet, be one.

So, if being an alpha bitch isn't going to help you attract and marry a mega-rich celebrity or some other great guy, what else should you do?

First, change your mindset about femininity itself. Stop equating it with weakness and confusing a legitimate quest for equal justice under the law and success in the workplace with a counterproductive quest for equality with men in *all* things. Men and women are genetically different. (I realize that the distinction may not be obvious in Seattle and San Francisco, but trust me on this one). We're not exactly the same and never will be. Accept it and focus instead on being the best, non-bitchy woman you can be.

Second, look for ways that Keepers express their natural femininity and allow their men to be masculine. Then copy some of those behaviors and incorporate them into your routine until they become second-nature. You will soon discover that simple courtesies—little things that you'd do without thinking if you weren't so busy trying to be masculine—work wonders. I'm not going to use this space for a laundry list of examples, and I shouldn't have to. You know what to do, and if you're not sure, watch the Keepers.

Be sure to notice what Keepers *don't* do and say around men as well because eliminating off-putting alpha-bitch behaviors can be as important as adding some new confidently feminine ones. Soon, you'll be a fully loaded, confident, highly feminine, American Keeper... whether or not you choose to spend part of your day in a boardroom. It's not a zero-sum game.

Third, learn to flirt. Flirtatiousness is a Southern tradition, but women in many other parts of the country apparently didn't get the memo. That's unfortunate because men love women who know how to flirt, and Keepers tend to do it in a cute, sexy, welcoming way that makes a man want to approach, even if he's shy. (They're highly unlikely to make the first move, however, because that's a man's job.) This kind of flirting is hard to resist and—for most guys—can't happen often enough. Dating site winks and social media pokes aren't the same. Anyone can do that.

If flirting makes you uncomfortable, maybe all you need is a new move. Watch how Keepers flirt—in person or via YouTube—and look for something new that might work for you. Read some books and articles on the subject, too. I just Googled "flirting" and found "11 Pretty Cool Things You Didn't Know About Flirting," for example. Not bad.

Then take some chances out there. Don't go overboard, but don't worry so much about rejection and failure either. I can't think of a single occasion in my entire life when a woman flirted with me and I wasn't flattered.

Keeper Principle #7:
Respect Good and Decent
Men—Broadly Defined
(Stop Routinely Hating and Disrespecting Men)

Rodney Dangerfield was known for the catchphrase "I don't get no respect!" and his comedic monologues on that theme. He was hilarious, but most men who say that about you won't stick around long if they have a choice.

If you routinely disrespect, dislike or hate men—even if you think you can focus all of your vitriol on "privileged" white heterosexual males or another subset of the gender that you despise for some stupid reason—and it's reflected in the things you say and do, *nothing else matters*. You can do everything else right and still lose a great guy if you emasculate him for any extended period of time. He doesn't need you in his life to do that.

Men want and need to feel important, valued, and respected in a relationship. It's in our DNA. So, if you've got a good man, do and say little things to make him feel that way. That's not asking too much, is it? If he doesn't feel like a man, he won't act like one, and there's a Keeper around the corner who'd be more than happy to step in and rectify the situation.

I acknowledge that a tiny minority of men get off on being treated like shit, at least once in a while. I have two friends in Los Angeles who worked part-time as dominatrices several years ago. (No, I was never a client. Relax.) Each told me shocking stories about guys who'd come to them for verbal abuse and, to a much lesser extent, physical pain. (One gal did the whole thing over Skype. "Fix your tutu! Now, dance around like a ballerina! You're a loser! You'll never get a girl like me!" "You're disgusting!"

They claimed at least 80% of their clients were wealthy (mostly Jewish) men who were masters of their domain at the office. Go figure.

So yes, there are oddballs out there if that's what you want, but most guys want no part of this dominatrix crap. They want to be loved and respected by a Keeper, and there's no fucking way they'd ever wear a tutu.

Keeper Principle #8:
Welcome and Appreciate Attention from Men
(Don't Be a Cold Bitch)

Keepers tend to encourage, expect and welcome attention from men, even when there are mild sexual overtones. They appreciate compliments too, as long as the guy offering them does so respectfully. Keepers may not be easy to meet and get to know in many situations, but they're always more friendly and approachable than American feminists, bitches, and other women with a grudge against men, especially outside of the Southern States.

Even celebrity Keepers like Shakira make an effort to genuinely appreciate attention from male fans who approach politely. One of my American buddies was at an airport a few years ago when she arrived with her entourage. Since he was a fan, he walked up to her at the Baggage Claim and said something complimentary, even though he normally wouldn't do such a thing. Many female celebrities would have given him a half-smile or barely audible "thank you" and either quickly turn away or signal for a bodyguard to intervene. Not Shakira. The conversation didn't last long, but she was extremely friendly and down-to-earth the whole time, as if her fame was no big deal and she appreciated her fans. My friend was delighted and couldn't get over how nice she was. He will never forget it.

Men don't love and marry bitches with a hostile, defensive, standoffish attitude, as if they're too busy or important to acknowledge the attention they get. Men love and marry women who are confident and comfortable enough to appreciate and welcome attention from men who find them attractive and secure enough to handle jerks who don't keep a respectful distance, say something rude, or otherwise abuse the privilege.

I know it's not easy to deal with strangers who call out or approach you at times, and some guys definitely need to be put in their place, at least. (I would never let a guy treat either of my younger sisters disrespectfully, for example.) But try to handle the others in stride, preferably with a smile.

You never know who might walk up next.

Keeper Principle #9:
Make Men Wait and Work for Sex
(Don't Be a Shameless, Manly Slut)

Keepers may dress provocatively and look sexy most of the time, but they normally aren't as slutty or promiscuous as American feminists and bitches, and it works to their advantage with men. There are regional and cultural variations of course, but Keepers tend to make guys wait and work for sex, and they give them plenty of rope to hang themselves in the interim.

You should follow suit. If a guy won't wait *at least* a month for sex from the day you start dating, he's just not that into you. He wouldn't give up so easily if he was. That may be difficult to believe in light of America's hook-up culture, but guys are just playing the game that so many women apparently want to play, and enjoying it as best they can. You don't have to participate, and you shouldn't if you're looking for a serious relationship.

You can make rare exceptions to the longer waiting period if there's sensational chemistry, if you're incredibly lonely (or horny), or if I'm involved (just kidding! sort of), but otherwise stick to your guns and make him sweat it out. If you don't think sex with you is a big deal and act accordingly, he won't either, and that's not going to help you find love or marriage.

There's nothing inherently strange or bitchy about making a guy work and wait a while for sex. You need time to get to know who he really is. And once you extend the waiting period for a month or so, the odds of him screwing things up increase significantly, and that's not a bad thing. If he does something wrong or hurtful, you'll be glad you haven't closed the deal yet. So will the next guy who comes along, who may be far more compatible with you. He may even be the One.

Hey, if you won't believe me, how about Sherry Argov, author of *Why Men Love Bitches?* She's not right about much, and her underlying logic is flawed, but we agree on this. She advises her reader to keep it platonic for the first month of dating and wait as long as possible before having sex.

Even a broken clock is right twice a day.

Keeper Principle #10:
Place a Higher Value on Family
(Don't Raise Red Flags)

Keepers generally place family at or near the top of their priority list, even if they're successful in business or a profession.

Men love it, even if they're not particularly family-oriented themselves because women who believe strongly in family and traditional values are more likely to treat them lovingly and respectfully in a relationship and raise happy, stable, well-balanced children. They're also less likely to cheat, file for a divorce, or run off with the kids and half of the family's assets.

Many feminists bristle at the suggestion that they should be more family-oriented. Some object because they had a lousy upbringing themselves. Others think "family-oriented" and "family values" are code words for losing their independence, earning capacity, career, or "reproductive rights" to become stay-at-home moms. Well, I'm not using code words in this book and don't see it that way.

Contrary to what you see and hear in much of the media today, most men like it when a woman has something that she's passionate about besides her boyfriend or husband. It makes her more interesting and sexy, and the extra money generated (if any) can make it easier to live larger or travel more together. However, if a woman's career overshadows her family life to the point where she could take it or leave it, men start to wonder about whether it makes sense to become the newest member of a dysfunctional family.

Tragically, many women utter the right clichés about the importance of family but ultimately screw their men anyway. It's as if the concept of "family" doesn't necessarily include the man, especially after a kid or two, when he's served his purpose and can henceforth be replaced, ignored or fleeced in court. I know that most of you aren't like this, but it happens often enough to make (American) guys seriously question the true importance of family—or, more specifically, a husband—to American women. Some men boycott American women altogether because of this.

It's a big, bright red flag that you don't want to wave.

So, what should you do? Behave as if family matters to you and there's a key role for a good man to play in yours, even if you're a busy career woman. Show him that your concept of family doesn't revolve solely around kids and parents or grandparents. You understand the importance of a great boyfriend and husband, too. Guys pick up on this stuff, and it affects the choices they make about whom to love and marry, and whom to leave behind.

Keeper Principle #11:
Show Him that You're Different
(Don't Expect Men to Believe What You Say)

This Principle isn't called "*Tell* Him that You're Different" because actions speak louder than words, and too many women say meaningless things that guys have learned to ignore, especially on dating apps and websites. If you want great men to love and marry you, you need to *show* them that you're different from bitches with a chip on their shoulder, ulterior motives, and heavy baggage out the wazoo. Talk is cheap.

After listening to and dealing with shrill third-wave feminists and whiny social justice warriors for so long, many men have a pre-conceived notion that American women are ultimately going to disappoint, reject, bankrupt, belittle, or otherwise emasculate them. I call it the relationship equivalent of post-traumatic stress syndrome. But don't worry. If you really are different, you can snap him out of it pretty easily, and you can do it in a nice way. There's always a workaround, and there's no need to be a bitch. Resorting to bitchiness will only amplify the problem and push him away.

Try this instead: Show him that you know how to dress, talk, and act like a Keeper. Show him that you like and respect decent men, even when you disagree from time to time. Show him that you're warm, friendly, and approachable but expect to be treated like a princess at all times. And show him that you don't use sex to trap or manipulate men or mindlessly sleep with every guy who survives three dates or less.

Works like a charm... if you are, in fact, different.

Keeper Principle #12:
Mind Your Own Business
(Ignore the Losers and Haters)

Men can be difficult. There are some real liars, jerks, and hateful trolls out there. I get it, trust me. I'm not making excuses for them and neither should you. But they shouldn't matter because they're not your problem.

You should be narrowly focused on attracting, getting, and keeping a really *great* guy, and the only way to do that is to mind your own business—physical, mental, emotional, and spiritual—and do things that maximize your likelihood of success. My mother puts it this way, "Mind your own business. And what other people think of you is not your business."

Now I'm not suggesting that you adopt a bitchy attitude and expect guys to accept you as you are without making an effort. That's not minding your own business; that's quitting and letting yourself go. It's what militant feminists and other losers do, and it's almost always coupled with male-bashing, whining, and complaining that will make you look even worse.

If you strive to be the best you can be and some guy comes along who still isn't impressed, that's not your business, either; it's his. There's no accounting for taste. You may learn something that helps you to attract and get a similar guy next time, and those are valuable lessons, but there's no sense in beating yourself (or him) up over it.

Keep your head up and focus on what you can control and improve—your business. There are plenty of eligible bachelors who are looking for a Keeper who can handle men and life in stride, with a laugh and a smile. It conveys confidence—not bitchiness—and it attracts men. Good ones.

Keeper Principle #13:
Send the Right Cues
(Don't Expect Him to Understand You)

According to Jerry Seinfeld, "Men want the same thing from their underwear that they want from women: a little bit of support, and a little bit of freedom." There's some truth in that joke, as in all good comedy. Men are simple. They're just not *that* simple. You gotta keep an eye on them, set some boundaries, and send the right cues about what you expect from the relationship.

Keepers aren't demanding and emasculating like feminists, but they don't hesitate to educate their men in a (mostly) loving way about acceptable and unacceptable behavior. If men are from Mars and women are from Venus, and you aren't interested in moving to Mars–no self-respecting Keeper switches planets–you should anticipate some misunderstandings from time to time, and take steps to minimize the damage they cause. (He should too, of course.) Even the best guys will step on a landmine once in a while unless you tell them where they're hidden in advance.

And remember: Even after you're more of a Keeper than you've ever been, the game ain't over. As long as your relationship continues, he'll be taking cues from you. Make them good ones.

Oh, and don't be a bitch about it.

Keeper Principle #14:
Develop and Cultivate the Habits of a Keeper
(Don't Stay in Your Comfort Zone)

In the movie *Grand Canyon,* there's a great scene about how we persevere and forge ahead in the face of hardship. Over breakfast,

Simon (Danny Glover) tells Mack (Kevin Kline) about his father's worn, rugged face:

> Simon: When I used to look at that face, and see all the pain there, all the things he lost, all the hurt he had, I wondered why he wanted to go on, why he just didn't lay down and give it up.
>
> Mack: Did you figure it out?
>
> Simon: No. Never figured out much about that guy. I asked him though.
>
> Mack: What did he say?
>
> Simon: Habit.

Good habits don't just help us survive. They increase our likelihood of success in all areas of life and help us to enjoy the journey more as well.

My grandmother Kitty Howe ("Gram"), who was 99 when she passed away a few years ago, was truly delightful. She had aches and pains, stress, anxiety, and other problems like the rest of us, and there were times when she expressed a strong opinion about this or that, but there was always a smile and laugh ready to go. Everyone loved her.

One day, I thought about that scene from the movie *City Slickers* when Billy Crystal ("Mitch") asks Jack Palance ("Curly") what the secret to life is. I decided to ask Gram the same question. After all, whatever it was, it seemed to be working for her. She just giggled and said: "Oh, just be happy and laugh a lot." I was a little disappointed with that answer at first because I expected something more profound, but then it hit me. By thinking and living that way each day, she'd developed a habit of happiness and laughter. She was habitually happy and cheerful, even as she playfully joked and flirted with hunky paramedics who took her to the hospital on her last day.

Not such a bad way to live, is it?

Don't stay in your comfort zone and settle for living like a humorless bitch or man-hating feminist. Keepers jettison habits that reinforce bad attitudes like that and cultivate new ones that enhance their confidence, femininity, sense of humor, and happiness. You can, too.

Keeper Principle #15:
Do the Opposite Temporarily, If Necessary (Never Give Up)

What if you've applied the previous 14 Keeper Principles and nothing changes? You still feel unappreciated, unattractive, or even invisible at times, and your relationships with men aren't improving significantly.

In that case, as a last resort, do "The Opposite."

The Opposite Principle is based on a famous episode of *Seinfeld*, where George Costanza and Jerry Seinfeld had the following exchange:

> George: "My life is the complete opposite of everything I want it to be. Every instinct I have in every aspect of my life, be it something to wear, something to eat... It's often wrong."

> Jerry: "If every instinct you have is wrong, then the opposite would have to be right."

George thought that insight was brilliant. All he needed to do to turn his life around was *the exact opposite* of every instinct, habit, tendency or inclination he had at that time.

Then, sure enough, George transformed from a lonely, unemployed loser living with his parents into a magnetic ladies man working as a high-priced executive for the New York Yankees before the 22-minute show was over.

I realize of course that *Seinfeld* is just a really good TV sitcom, but doing the opposite of whatever you're doing right now may be the shock therapy you need to get out of your rut and open your mind to other alternatives.

Steve Sample, in his bestselling book, *The Contrarian's Guide to Leadership,* offered some similar wisdom about application of the Opposite Principle from a somewhat more authoritative source, Aristotle:

> "Aristotle noted that, when carpenters wish to straighten a warped board, they don't put it in a jip that simply holds it straight; rather they put it in a jig that bends it in the opposite direction from that in which it is warped. After a week or two in this reverse-bending configuration, the board naturally springs back to a straight shape when it is released from the jig. So it is when we attempt to correct our own weaknesses. We must bend over backward in an effort to overcompensate, and in that way we just might achieve a reasonable middle ground."

What does this mean for you? It depends on who you are now and what you've been doing. If you're a bitch who's hoping to become a Keeper—good for you—then you've got to act on the opposite of every bitchy impulse for a while by being the sweetest girl in town. If you're a slut who's tired of being screwed and discarded by one guy after another, it's time to start saying "No" to casual sex and reserving intimacy for special men who wait, work for, and earn it. Sorry.

And yes, if you're one of those women who really are "too nice" to men—I'd call it "too stupid" because I don't consider niceness as a liability, but whatever—then you'll have to be a lot more selfish for a while. Call it bitchier if you want, but remember this: If you don't spring back to a pleasant, sensible middle ground within a reasonable period of time, you'll defeat the purpose of this exercise and create new problems for yourself. You can irreparably damage your friendships and reputation, too.

It's just not worth it. There are already too many bitches to go around.

Be a Keeper whom men love and marry, instead.

**YOU READ THE BOOK.
NOW, GET THE LOOK.**

Available only at
www.bitchologystore.com.

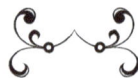

Conclusion

*"I suggest you stop whining like a little bitch...
and do what I say."*

— JESSIE PINKMAN, *BREAKING BAD*

Thank you for reading this book. I appreciate your interest in bitchology and the truth about who men love and marry.

I've done my best to show you that third-wave feminists and social justice warriors are lying to you about the appeal and consequences of bitchiness. If you think you're "too nice" to succeed with men, trying to look, talk, and act like more of a bitch is only going to make things worse.

As it turns out, the choice between being a submissive doormat and a nasty bitch is a false one. You lose either way, but there's another approach to attracting, getting, and keeping a great guy that works like a charm.

My years of research and extensive life experience reveal that America's best men are looking for a different kind of woman—a *confidently feminine* one or a "Keeper"—and Keepers are in short supply in many parts of the country these days. Feminists may be loud, opinionated and pushy, but most are actually neither confident nor feminine. Other American women may be strong in one area but weak in the other. The key to success with America's best men is an abundance of both—confidence *and* femininity.

I outlined 15 "Keeper Principles" in chapter 6 of this book to help you do an even better job of turning the heads and winning the hearts of high-quality men. You can choose to dismiss them and stay in your comfort zone, but nothing is going to change if you keep doing the same things. You have to take a chance, even if it's scary at times, and try something new. If some of the principles don't work for or appeal to you for some reason, no worries. Stick with the ones that do and modify them to suit your needs.

I hope this book inspires you to become the best Keeper you can be and encourage your daughters and girlfriends to do the same. And I hope it helps you to better understand, attract, get, and keep a truly great guy.

If you'd like to continue the discussion–I don't profess to have all of the answers and appreciate your feedback, as long as it's rational–contact me anytime on my website (JoeBovino.com), Twitter (@joebovino), Facebook (joebovinopage), LinkedIn (joebovino), or Instagram (@realjoebovino).

And, if you'd like some guidance in turning your own expertise, wisdom or great idea into a bestselling book of your own, schedule a free strategy session with me or one of my colleagues at Bestseller in You Publishing (BestsellerInYou.com). We look forward to hearing from you.

Later, bitches! ;)

Credits

EDITING

Diane Chesson, PhD, MBA (diane.chesson@gmail.com) provided
editing and proofreading services.

BOOK DESIGN

iPublicidades (https://www.elance.com/s/speedread) provided
book layout and design, cover design, logo design, and eBook
conversion services.

ILLUSTRATIONS

Linda Jackson and Darren Jackson of DarlinDesign (darlindesign.co.uk)
provided the following illustrations: Boca Bitch, Hole in One, and
So Ho'.

Carsten Mell (carstenmell.com) provided the following illustrations:
49er, Bigger Better Deal, Big Sister, Bronx Tail, Cougar, Hurt
Rocker, Nuyorican, Perfect 6, Sili-Clone and South Beeotch.

Gerben den Heeten of Gerb-Art (gerb-art.com) provided the Brooding
Barfly illustration.

About The Author

APPEARANCE: There he is.

VOICE: His own, like it or not.

BEHAVIOR: Loves to turn ideas into bestselling books. Practices law, too. Enjoys people watching, especially chickspotting and chicaspotting, working out, cross-cultural affairs (in various forms), history, politics, music, and satire.

MATING: Loves women more than Fabio, except for the bitches. More player-coach than player these days. Master of international relations. (Well, not exactly, but he does have a master's degree in international relations from USC.) Loyal and ready to settle down but prepared to stay single if necessary, at least until he's too old to feed himself. Gold medalist in bed, no matter what she says.

MAGNETS: Prefers extraordinary women (who love his books and think he's awesome) to ordinary ones (who don't). No mustache is a plus. Irritable bowel syndrome and third-wave feminism are deal breakers.

For more information about the author, visit JoeBovino.com.

Notes

Introduction

Helen Smith, PhD, *Men on Strike: Why Men Are Boycotting Marriage, Fatherhood, and the American Dream – and Why It Matters* (Encounter Books, 2013).

Erin Gloria Ryan, "The United States of Bros: A Map and Field Guide" *Jezebel* (April 2, 2014), http://jezebel.com/the-united-states-of-bros-a-map-and-field-guide-1550563737 (Retrieved September 5, 2016).

Erin Gloria Ryan, "The United States of Basic Bitches: A Map and Field Guide" *Jezebel* (June 30, 2014), http://jezebel.com/the-united-states-of-basic-bitches-1575949216 (Retrieved September 5, 2016).

Lindy West, "The 92 'Species' of Women According to an Incredibly Stupid Dude from a P90X Video," *Jezebel* (May 8, 2012) http://jezebel.com/5908451/the-92-species-of-women-according-to-one-incredibly-stupid-dude (Retrieved January 2, 2015).

Emma Gray, "Joe Bovino's Field Guide to Chicks May Be Worst Book Ever," *Jezebel* (May 9, 2012), http://www.huffingtonpost.com/emma-gray/joe-bovino-field-guide-to-chicks-of-the-united-states-worst-book-ever_b_1504416.html (Retrieved January 2, 2015).

Chapter One: FEMININITY ≠ WEAKNESS

David Nash, "Milo: Feminists 'Waging War on Working-Class Men,'" *Breitbart* (February 18, 2016). http://www.breitbart.com/tech/2016/02/18/milo-feminists-are-waging-war-on-working-class-men (Retrieved August 13, 2016).

"An Interview with Julie Bindel," *Radfem Collective: Positively Revolting Women* (September 7, 2015). http://www.radfemcollective.org/news/2015/9/7/an-interview-with-julie-bindel (Retrieved August 13, 2015).

Sherry Argov, *Why Men Love Bitches: From Doormat to Dreamgirl – A Woman's Guide to Holding Her Own in a Relationship* (Adams Media, 2009), pgs. xiv, xvi, 6, 9, 14, 17, 19, 20, 23, 44, 50, 57, 61, 69, 73, 99, 112, 116, 123, 146, 185, 212, 216, 230, and 233.

Gigi Engle, "24 Reasons Nice Guys Always Chase The B*tch – As Told By The B*tch," *Elite Daily* (December 16, 2014), http://elitedaily.com/dating/nice-guys-always-chase/882130 (Retrieved January 2, 2015).

Chapter Two: THIRD-WAVE FEMINISM: WAVE GOODBYE TO GOOD MEN

Kara Brown, "Watch a Woman Experience 100 Instances of Street Harassment in One Day," *Jezebel* (October 28, 2014), http://jezebel.com/watch-a-woman-experience-100-instances-of-street-harass-165180 (Retrieved December 2, 2014).

Susan Schorn, "How to Kick a Guy in the Balls: An Illustrated Guide," *Jezebel* (November 12, 2014), http://jezebel.com/how-to-kick-a-guy-in-the-balls-an-illustrated-guide- 1657810297 (Retrieved December 20, 2014).

Lena Dunham, "The Lenny Interview: Amy Schumer," *Lenny* (September 2, 2016), http://www.lennyletter.com/culture/interviews/a527/the-lenny-interview-amy-schumer (Retrieved September 4, 2016).

Sara Jones and Jennifer Pearson, "'I'm so sorry... I shouldn't have acted like I did.': Lena Dunham apologises to Odell Beckham, Jr. for accusing him of ignoring her at Met Gala," *DailyMail.com* (September 3, 2016), http://www.dailymail.co.uk/tvshowbiz/article-3772554/Lena-Dunham-apologises-Odell-Beckham-Jr-accusing-ignoring-Met-Gala.html (Retrieved September 4, 2016).

Chapter Three: KARMA IS A BITCH

Reannon Muth, "No Sex in the City: What It's Like to Be Single and Foreign in Japan," *Vagabondish* (March 5, 2013), http://www.vagabondish.com/female-foreign-japan (Retrieved January 2, 2015).

Reannon Muth, "Are North American Women Really THAT Bad," *Taken By The Wind,* http://www.takenbythewind.com/2010/09/17/are-north-american-women-really-that-bad (Retrieved January 5, 2015).

Chapter Four: A LITTLE SHAME GOES A LONG WAY

Milo Yiannopoulos, "Science Proves It: Fat-Shaming Works," *Breitbart* (July 5, 2016). http://www.breitbart.com/milo/2016/07/05/fat-shaming-is-good-science (Retrieved August 12, 2016).

Chad D. Jensen, Kara M. Duraccio, Sanita l. Hunsaker, Diana Rancourt, Elizabeth S. Kuhl, Elissa Jelalian, and Rena R. Wing, "A Qualitative Study of Successful Adolescent and Young Adult Weight Losers: Implications for Weight Control Intervention," *Childhood Obesity* Volume 10, Issue 6, pages 482-490 (2014).

Daniel Callahan, "Obesity: Chasing an Elusive Epidemic," *Hastings Center Report,* 2013 Jan-Feb;43(1):34-40. doi: 10.1002/hast.114. Epub 2012 Dec 18.

Dossie Easton and Janet W. Hardy, *The Ethical Slut: A Practical Guide to Polyamory, Open Relationships and Other Adventures* (Celestial Arts, 2009).

Chapter Five: BITCHSPOTTING: AIN'T THAT A BITCH

Alexis De Tocqueville, *Democracy in America*. Trans. Mansfield, Harvey C. and Delba Winthrop. Chicago: University of Chicago Press, 2000, Volume 2 Part 3, Chapter 12, page 573-574)

Euro-Mina

James Bracken, *Che Boludo! A gringo's guide to understanding the Argentines,* Editorial Caleuche (2005).

"Argentine American," *Wikipedia, The Free Encyclopedia.* http://en.wikipedia.org/wiki/Argentine_American (Retrieved February 3, 2012).

"List of Argentine Americans," *Wikipedia, the Free Encyclopedia* http://en.wikipedia.org/wiki/List_of_Argentine_Americans (Retrieved November 25, 2014).

Nuyorican

Movieline, October 1996.

"Jennifer Lopez: 'Skinny Girls Miss Out'" (citing quote to *New York Post*), *US Weekly* (January 8, 2010). http://www.usmagazine. com/healthylifestyle/news/jennifer-lopez-skinny-girls-miss-out-201081 (Retrieved May 10, 2010).

See also "Jennifer Lopez," *AskMen;* http://www.askmen.com/celebs/ women/singer/3_jennifer_lopez.html (Retrieved May 10, 2010).

"List of Stateside Puerto Ricans," *Wikipedia, the Free Encyclopedia* http://en.wikipedia.org/wiki/List_of_Stateside_Puerto_Ricans (Retrieved November 26, 2014).

"Nuyorican," *Wikipedia, The Free Encyclopedia.* http://en.wikipedia. org/wiki/Nuyorican (Retrieved May 10, 2010).

49er

"Freeboobing," *Urbandictionary.com.* http://www.urbandictionary.com/ define.php?term=freeboobing (Retrieved January 5, 2012).

Sili-Clone

"Map of Orange County Beaches," Lonelyplanet.com.
   http://www.lonelyplanet.com/maps/north-america/usa/
   orangecounty- beaches (Retrieved May 8, 2010).

Perfect 6

"America's Best (and Worst) Cities for Dating," Sperling's BestPlaces.
   http://www.bestplaces.net/docs/studies/DatingCities.aspx
   (Retrieved May 8, 2010).

Hurt Rocker

"The Emo Hangout," Emo Corner. http://www.emo-corner.com/emo-
   girls-pictures (Retrieved April 27, 2010).
Uncyclopedia, Emo, http://uncyclopedia.wikia.com/wiki/Emo
   (Retrieved May 8, 2010).
"How to Get an Emo Girlfriend," wikiHow. http://www.wikihow.com/
   Get-an-Emo-Girlfriend (Retrieved May 8, 2010).
"Straight Edge," Wikipedia, The Free Encyclopedia.
   http://en.wikipedia.org/wiki/Straight_edge (Retrieved May 8, 2010).

Brooding Barfly

For a more in-depth analysis of hipster subculture, see Brenna Ehrlich
   and Andrea Bartz, Stuff Hipsters Hate: A Field Guide To The
   Passionate Opinions Of The Indifferent (Ulysses Press, 2010),
   and Robert Lanham, The Hipster Handbook (First Anchor Books
   Edition, February 2003). I relied on each of these books for
   insights into the subculture.
"How to Be a Hipster," wikiHow. http://www.wikihow.com/
   Be-a-Hipster (Retrieved September 20, 2011).
"Hipster," Urbandictionary.com. http://www.urbandictionary.com/
   define.php?term=hipster (Retrieved September 23, 2011).

Cougar

College Times. http://collegetimes.us/top-5-cougar-towns (Retrieved September 9, 2011).

Chapter Six: THE KEEPER PRINCIPLES

Kristen Houghton, "The New Trophy Wife," Huff Post Women (December 13, 2014), http://www.huffingtonpost.com/kristen-houghton/the-new-trophy-wife_b_6207364.html (Retrieved December 19, 2014).

Amanda Chatel, "11 Pretty Cool Things You Didn't Know About Flirting," Yahoo Style (January 3, 2015) https://www.yahoo.com/style/11-pretty-cool-things-you-didnt-know-about-106616804873.html (Retrieved January 3, 2015).

Joe Bovino, Field Guide to Chicks of the United States (Chickspotting, LLC, 2012), pgs. 147 and 167.

Rob Asghar, "Do The Opposite: Seinfeldian Wisdom For A Brighter New Year," Forbes (December 30, 2013), http://www.forbes.com/sites/robasghar/2013/12/30/do-the-opposite-seinfeldian-wisdom-for-a-brighter-new-year (Retrieved January 7, 2015).

Steven P. Sample, The Contrarian's Guide to Leadership (Jossey-Bass 2003).

Karen Salmansohn's How to Make Your Man Behave in 21 Days or Less Using the Secrets of Professional Dog Trainers, (Workman Publishing Company, 1994).